Bake

TRADITIONAL IRISH BAKING WITH MODERN TWISTS

Graham Herterich

NINE BEAN ROWS

Dedication

Daithí, thank you for your continued love, support and encouragement.
Pappy, thank you for your friendship, inspiration and the joy you
bring to my life. I love you both so much.

Contents

Acknowledging the women
who inspired & inspire

Many of my food memories in this book are centred around the wonderful women in my life growing up. Each of these women cooked and baked with real love and passion and you could taste it in every bite. There are many people who made me the baker I am today, but I want to thank the following women in particular.

My mum, Ann Herterich, who saw, encouraged and supported my love of food and baking. She introduced me to most of the classics in this book.

My sister, Ingrid – Swiss rolls and fudge

Granny Flynn – traditional tea brack

Granny Daisy – guggy, one-sided toast and milk jelly

Aunty Mary – Christmas cakes, puddings and pavlova

Mrs Tobin – curnie cake

Ruth Coyle – seasonal tarts

Mrs Supple – soda bread

Mrs Bergin – chocolate cheesecake and hostess trolly meringue

Olive Perry – coffee cake

Mairead Hutchinson – trifle and chocolate pudding

Monica Kelleher – fruit cakes, porter cake and tarts, and in recent years she has reminded me of the joys of baking

I also want to recognise some of the amazing women in Irish food who continue to inspire me on a daily basis, from chefs like Jess Murphy, Gráinne O'Keefe and Aoife Noonan and producers like Siobhán Ní Ghairbhith (St Tola), Birgitta Hedin-Curtin (Burren Smokehouse) and Sheila Butler (Cuinneog) to writers like Dee Laffan and Ali Dunworth who have contributed to this book and food champions like Dr Sally McKenna and Fallon Moore. I don't intend this to be a comprehensive list in any way because there are so many talented women in the Irish food scene, but it is an example of the awesome women in Ireland's food industry.

Of course I can't forget the wonderful all-woman team behind this book. Thank you to Kristin Jensen, Jane Matthews, Orla Neligan and Jo Murphy for making my dream a reality.

Introduction

MOST OF THE TIME I CAN'T REMEMBER WHAT I DID YESTERDAY, BUT WHILE WRITING THIS BOOK, I'VE UNLOCKED SO MANY MEMORIES. THIS BOOK HAS BECOME MORE THAN JUST A COLLECTION OF RECIPES. IT'S A LOOK BACK AT THE MANY PEOPLE, THE MAJORITY OF WHOM ARE WOMEN, WHO HAVE INFLUENCED MY LIFE, MY CAREER AND MY PASSION FOR FOOD. IT'S MADE ME REALISE HOW POWERFUL FOOD IS AS A CONNECTION TO OUR PAST AND TO OTHER PEOPLE.

I was born in Athy, County Kildare in December 1977 and grew up in Number 4 Duke Street over the family's pork butcher shop that bore our Herterich family name. My grandfather, Ernest Herterich, opened the shop in February 1942. I heard great things about him as I grew up, but unfortunately I never met him as he died at a young age in 1967.

I'm the middle child of five, with an older brother and sister and two younger brothers. Our mother was, and still is, a fantastic cook, so we grew up eating good, wholesome, fresh, homemade food. I remember on one occasion going to a friend's house and having a Findus Crispy Pancake for dinner. I couldn't get over how good it tasted (at the time) and wondered why we never had them at home. When I look back now, I don't think we knew how lucky we were.

Living over the shop, us kids always had little jobs to do growing up, from weighing seasonings for sausages to helping Bobby, my dad's uncle and one of the butchers, tie the sausages as well as pressing hams, brining meats and the big clean-down on Saturday evening. We would watch in awe as my father and the other butchers boned out the meat.

Mum's friends were all fantastic cooks and I have so many memories of these women calling to our house. They would drop in for a cuppa and a chat and would bring something they had baked at home with them. Myself and my brother Claude would patiently wait upstairs for them to leave so that we could rush down to see what delectable delights they had brought.

During the summer of 1991 I was lucky enough to spend a few weeks with my sister Ingrid, who was living and studying in Camden Town in London. That trip was a culture shock that really opened my 13-year-old eyes. I will always remember my sister telling me to close my mouth when we were on the Underground travelling from the airport to Camden. I was a young boy from Kildare and I'd never seen so many people of different ethnic backgrounds, which was amplified when we explored the bustling Camden markets with their treasure troves of colourful clothing and foods and flavours I had never experienced before.

That trip was also a culture shock in another way: I discovered art. The bus from Camden stopped on Trafalgar Square, home of the National Gallery, where I spent many days discovering the wonderful world of art. I spent hours walking around the gallery, particularly entranced by *Vase with Fifteen Sunflowers* by Vincent van Gogh. I was also mesmerised by a painting by Harmen Steenwyck called *Still Life: An Allegory of the Vanities of Human Life*. During that trip I also went to my first concert – not many people can say that their first concert was Luciano Pavarotti in Hyde Park. I will never forget that rainy day in July 1991 for so many good reasons, not least the music, the atmosphere and a distant glimpse of Princess Diana. We got there around 8:30 in the morning and from then on there was a growing buzz of good humour and anticipation, even when the heavens opened. Pavarotti took to the stage that evening and his presence and voice commanded the 100,000-strong audience from the beginning to the closing note.

butcher shop other than my father's as well as a factory in Kilkenny where I made fresh soups. Most importantly, I got to work in Tonlegee House, a country house hotel and restaurant in Athy. It was during my time there working with Mark Molloy that my love of food really developed. He took me under his wing and encouraged my growing interest in food.

I went on to study culinary arts under the CERT Programme in Waterford. While studying, I was able to work in amazing places like Kilkee Castle, the Pine Rooms, Marlfield House and Mount Juliet. I also did *stages* in great restaurants such as Chapter One, Peacock Alley and the Commons.

I absolutely loved what I was doing with my career, but there was something else, something that I had always wondered about, and that was religious life. So just as my career as a chef was about to start, I decided to enter the Carmelite community. I spent a brilliant two years in the order, a period of time that I will never regret.

'It was during my time working at Tonlegee House with Mark Molloy that my love of food really developed.'

I also took trips to work with the sick in Lourdes as a teenager, something I still do today. I and most of my family have done it for years, my father for as long as I can remember. While the work was rewarding, it was the food that really got my attention, whether it was sitting outside Café Au Roi Albert with my friend Tara enjoying French onion soup or a croque madame or wandering the local supermarket with my mum, discovering all the new ingredients and French foods. Southern French food, particularly that of the Pyrenees region, still has a place in my heart.

As a result of all these various influences, I have always had an interest in food, an interest that grew when I entered fourth year in secondary school. During work experience that year I worked in a

At the end of those two years I was feeling a little lost, so I decided to take a break and ended up going to Morocco on a cheap one-week sun package holiday. Using Agadir as a base, I wound up travelling around for almost four weeks, which even included a few days working as a goatherd. It was here that my love of food was reignited. I could not get enough b'ssara, tagine, couscous and mint tea, not to mention the buzz of Jemaa el-Fnaa in Marrakech and the many souks I visited. (To this day, I still love to spend time exploring souks and markets wherever I travel.) I was only 21 years old, but this trip was significant because on the plate it was a gateway to the foods of Morocco, Egypt, Palestine and the broad scope of Middle Eastern cuisine.

1 With Granny and Granddad Flynn at my christening 2 My sister Ingrid holding my brother Pappy with Ernie, Claude and me 3 Aunty Mary 4 On holiday in Courtown, Wexford 5 My mum 6 Me

When I returned from that holiday I decided that I didn't want to go back into religious life, but I didn't want to go back into the high-end restaurants I had been working in either. Instead, I decided to work in smaller establishments, which ultimately led to a career in product development and food production. I was made redundant in October 2012, but with the help of my partner, Daithí, and some amazing advice and support from someone who has always wanted to remain anonymous, I set up my own business, The Cupcake Bloke.

Over the past 10 years my business has given me the opportunity to explore my love of baking traditions and flavours, especially since we opened our first shop in 2018, The Bakery in Rialto. I've always been fascinated by taking classic Irish recipes and giving them a modern twist. By classic, I mean the it all started, as it's the first thing I learned to bake with my Granny Flynn when I was seven or eight years old. From there, I learned to enjoy food and flavour as well as how to reimagine and take risks reinventing bakes.

I don't claim to know everything when it comes to the history of Irish baking or the influx of new flavours to Ireland that have inspired so many of the newer interpretations in this book, so I have invited two people to contribute to this introduction. Ali Dunworth and Dee Laffan are both food writers, journalists and good friends of mine. Ali gives a brief introduction to Irish baking, while Dee introduces modern flavours and influences.

I want everyone to be able to take something from this book. If you are a first-time baker, I've included a section on pages 12–17 that will hopefully

'I've always been fascinated by taking classic Irish recipes and giving them a modern twist.'

proper Irish bakes like soda bread, tarts, porter cake and of course brack all the way up to modern classics like jambons, cheesecakes and fifteens.

The initial idea for this book was to show you some of these classic Irish bakes and then show you my modern interpretation of the same dish, but it also became a trip down the memory lane of my childhood, teens and early twenties all the way through to the last few years, when I became more confident in my decisions regarding food, flavours, inspirations and textures. As you go through this book you will see that every traditional bake is followed by a modern twist. It may not be an exact update of the recipe – it could be a modern interpretation of the flavour combination or a reinterpretation of the concept. But the heart of this book is the Brack & Butter chapter. Brack is where answer any questions you might have and give you the confidence to bake. If you have already started baking, I hope this book will give you some new ideas and techniques. Finally, if you are an accomplished baker or cook in the kitchen, I hope this book will encourage you to be adventurous, explore new flavours and develop your own modern classics (two books that I constantly go back to for inspiration are *The Flavour Thesaurus* by Niki Segnet and *The Science of Spice* by Stuart Farrimond).

I would love nothing more than for you and all the other people using this book to make your own memories by sharing your bakes with the people you love. You never know – a child you share a bake with or cook with could be remembering you when they write their first cookbook in 30 years.

Bácáil shona – happy baking!

1 Ingrid, Ernie, me and Claude 2 Pappy and me 3 Mrs Tobin and Granny Flynn 4 Daithí and me at our civil partnership, 29 June 2012 5 Mrs Tobin's house, Carolow 6 Granny Daisy on my christening day 7 Mum, me and Pappy on the Purple Run for Down Syndrome Ireland 8 Me and my dad in Israel

A brief history of Irish baking

BY ALI DUNWORTH

FRESH BAKING. JUST WRITING THE WORDS CAN EVOKE A SMILE, NOSTALGIA, PERHAPS EVEN AN URGE TO BITE INTO SOMETHING SWEET AND FLAKY. DID YOU CLOSE YOUR EYES AS YOU IMAGINED THE SMELL? THAT UNMISTAKABLE WAFT, THAT FIRST BITE, DELIVERS AN INSTANT DOSE OF SEROTONIN.

Traditional Irish baking may not be as famous as French boulangeries or Viennese patisserie, but baking, no matter how fancy, all began in the same way: as a daily ritual to keep folks fed. Early bread in Ireland was made with oats, but then wheat showed up with the Anglo-Normans and eventually bread soda, so by the mid-19th century soda bread – or cake, as it was more commonly known – was well on its way to becoming a staple in every Irish home. It was practical, nourishing and yeastless, raised with the buttermilk most houses had access to. Kitchens were functional and homely and so was the baking. You didn't need any special equipment to make soda bread, measurements were done by eye and you shaped it in a circle. You didn't even need a tin or oven – you could simply cook it in a pot on the fire. In a way, all the things we *didn't* have shaped the recipes we now come to think of as traditional baking.

Offering visitors or house callers tea and something to eat has always been the done thing in an Irish home, which is where scones would have come into their own. The fire would always be on and the simple ingredients for scones were always to hand, so they became the go-to partner for a simple bite with your tea. Cakes were baked too, but they were more for special occasions. They were rarely iced but often featured seasonal fruits like apples and blackberries when they were available or dried fruit and a dash of booze at other times. Recipes had to be simple and seasonal, which quickly becomes delicious and comforting when it shows up as scones, crumbles and cakes.

You can't talk about Irish baking without acknowledging folklore, of course. Don't forget to put a cross on top of your soda bread to let the fairies out or perhaps to ward off the devil from the house!

It's more likely that the cross helps the air to escape and your bread to cook more evenly, but where's the fun in that? When it comes to brack, everyone of a certain age in Ireland will remember the Halloween barmbrack and the fortune-telling fun you'd have if you came across the ring (marriage!) or the coin (wealth!). The year-round version of this loaf is simply called brack. It's still a moist fruit-filled loaf, just without the fortune-telling. The fruit, in fact, is where it gets its name. Brack *as Gaeilge* (in Irish) is *breac*

food lecturer and historian Máirtín Mac Con Iomaire in an effort to get to the bottom of where the name 'iced duck' comes from, but we concluded that a whole other book could be written on the etymology of Irish baking. Máirtín reminded me, 'It's such a small country, but you go down the road and we have different accents and then different names for bread and cakes.' A gur cake in one town is a donkey's gudge or Chester cake somewhere else. Graham's recipe for curnie cake is a version of soda bread also

'You can't talk about Irish baking without acknowledging folklore, of course. Don't forget to put a cross on top of your soda bread to let the fairies out.'

and means 'speckled', referring to the tea-soaked dried fruit that speckles this comforting traditional loaf. Every house would have had their own recipe, adapting and adjusting it according to what they had.

While plenty of our traditional Irish baking is domestic, usually passed down from grandmothers, mothers and aunts, we also have a tradition of local bakers. There are records of small commercial bakeries in Irish towns and villages going back to the mid-19th century. This was where you'd go for yeasted bread and cakes, Irish classics like batch loaves, turnovers and blaas. Bakeries like this still exist in towns and villages all over Ireland today. You know the places, full of pillowy white loaves; long, wide baguettes with rock-hard crusts and airy insides; cream cakes and slices galore; sweet confections; and classics like gur cakes – or is it a donkey's gudge? It all depends on what part of the country you're in.

Names were a great source of debate and amusement while researching this book. I chatted to

known as railway cake or spotted dog. What we would call a turnover in Dublin is known as a duck in Cork and a grinder in Galway. Could this be where the name iced duck came from? I didn't ever figure that out, but Graham has included an iced *duck* recipe in this book even though he only ever knew it as an iced *loaf*. But the duck name intrigued him so much that he played around with the recipe and came up with a thoroughly modern interpretation that he's called 'lucky duck'.

This thought process is exactly what makes Graham's baking so fascinating – he goes from deeply traditional to thoroughly modern. Get ready for a sweet slice of history packed with excellent recipes and heart-warming anecdotes.

The modern landscape of Irish food

BY DEE LAFFAN

TO UNDERSTAND GRAHAM'S ADAPTATIONS OF CLASSIC IRISH BAKING RECIPES AND HIS CHOICE OF DIFFERENT INGREDIENTS, SPICES AND INFLUENCES IS ALSO TO UNDERSTAND THE MODERN LANDSCAPE OF IRISH FOOD.

To comprehend where the influences and trends in Ireland are coming from, we need to take a deeper look at our growth in cultural diversity over the past few decades. Ireland's journey with immigration is still in its infancy, yet it has had a rapid growth spurt since the late 1990s. We went from a country of emigration to a country of immigration as we encouraged people to move here to sustain our Celtic Tiger economy. Our student visa policies targeted and attracted students from Asia, the Middle East and South America and our healthcare industry has a high number of doctors and nurses from India and the Philippines. We were one of the last EU countries to reach our migration turning point, yet now we have one of the highest proportions of immigrants in the EU. Today's largest minority population is Polish and the fastest-growing population is Brazilian. In fact, Ireland's population has recently risen above 5 million for the first time since 1851.

The rise in immigration has naturally led to a change in our foodscape, from restaurateurs and chefs to growers, producers and of course the products on our supermarket shelves. At the time of writing, a significant number of Ireland's Michelin-starred chefs hail from afar, including England, Finland, Japan, the Netherlands and Turkey; some of the best bakers in the country are from Argentina, Brazil, Hong Kong, Poland and Syria; Korean growing methods are being adopted by vegetable producers; top-quality Irish charcuterie – chorizo, bresaola and salami – is widespread; Ireland's first Mexican cookbook has been published; Irish Wagyu beef and buffalo mozzarella are now a speciality; a Malawi sauce range is being produced in Ireland and a Chinese-style peanut rayu has the foodie nation addicted; and Ireland has its first Ethiopian restaurant in Dublin. It's an exciting time!

Another reason for the influx of different cuisines is the fact that we are demanding them. Our tastes for spice and variety have been awoken. Irish people are avid global travellers, and influences from seasoned holidaymakers and those who've migrated back home after years living abroad are apparent. One of

Graham's favourite trips was to Israel and Palestine with his dad and he was really inspired by the food there. In fact, it's fair to say that Middle Eastern flavours feature the most in his recipes compared to other world regions.

Graham was led to his passion for Middle Eastern flavours from his love of North African food. It often happens that we start on a journey with one country's cuisine and through it, we find ourselves halfway across another continent while still in our own kitchen. By taking a deeper dive into Middle Eastern flavours, you'll have a better understanding of Graham's choices of spices and ingredients.

The food from Lebanon has a lot of warm, aniseed-flavoured spice profiles. I always think of mezze when I think of Lebanese food – a grazing course of small plates such as hummus, salad, olives, yogurt and dishes with eggs and vegetables that can lead to

page 208, which has to be tried to be believed!

One of the foods from Israel that I've noticed becoming more mainstream on a lot of Irish menus is zhug, an intensely spicy chilli paste that is actually Israel's national condiment. (I wonder what Ireland's national condiment is?) You can drizzle zhug on anything from falafel to your poached eggs in the morning. Sumac and za'atar are also ingredients that are becoming more common in the Irish larder. There are lots of versions of the latter – depending on the country, you have a slightly different mix of herbs and spices – but the Syrian version is fruity and sour and is divine sprinkled on labneh (strained yogurt) and vegetable dishes, especially aubergines. Sumac is a citrusy spice that adds a zingy hit to dishes, and Turkey is actually one of the leading producers of it. Try sprinkling it on hummus.

Moving to Persian spices such as advieh, Graham

'Middle Eastern spices are an important factor in the modern versions of recipes in this book, but Graham has also drawn a lot of inspiration from Asia.'

bigger dishes of grilled meat or a whole fish.

Turkey brings smoky, earthy flavours – think sujuk (spicy beef sausage) and tahini (check out the recipe for tahini and black sesame cupcakes on page 170) – and fresh ingredients like dates. Actually, Graham's malted coffee, chocolate and pecan brack (page 108) has a lot of Turkish flavours. Turkish coffee is unique in the way it's brewed and the malted coffee flavour in this brack reminds me of this. I also always associate pomegranates with Turkey. They are native to the country, but pomegranate molasses (nar eksisi), which can be used in marinades for meats or drizzled on salads, is what springs to mind. It is a truly beautiful ingredient that you can use like balsamic vinegar. One of the most fun recipes in this cookbook is the Buckfast, pomegranate and mint baked ham on

includes this in the Persian rice pudding on page 154. In fact, this recipe is quintessentially Middle Eastern, with rose and pistachio featuring too. Advieh is a spice blend of cardamom, cumin, cinnamon, ginger and rose and is often used for savoury rice, but here Graham uses it for a sweet dish, which is something he does often, and it works so well.

Graham includes the spice mahleb in his mahleb and orange shortbread on page 172. Mahleb cherry stones come from a tree that is native to the Mediterranean and the Middle East, including Greece, Turkey and North Africa. The seed within the cherry stone is dried and ground and used in baking but also in spice blends for dry rubs on meat. Apparently, if you add it to ice cream it gives it a wonderfully sweet and fruity (cherry) flavour and an almondy earthiness.

Middle Eastern spices are an important factor in the modern versions of recipes in this book, but Graham has also drawn a lot of inspiration from Asia. From South Asia, you'll find Indian influences in recipes such as the panch phoron soda bread on page 32. Panch phoran is a five-spice, whole spice mix from East India, particularly Bengal and Bangladesh. It's good for flavouring dahls and vegetable dishes. Graham's combination of this spice with onion in soda bread is the ultimate modern take on Irish soda and makes it incredibly moreish (you've been warned!).

There are lots of flavours from East Asia too. From China, South Korea and Japan, you'll see spices such as ginger and sesame being used and also ingredients such as miso, hoisin, enoki mushrooms and matcha. Of course, matcha originates in China but is regularly found in Japanese baking recipes. Does a bright green cake or Swiss roll ring any bells?

We are fortunate that nowadays the availability of flavours and accessibility of ingredients is a lot easier than it used to be. There is an international shop in most towns across the country, from Asian markets to Turkish or halal supermarkets, with shelves of spices, sauces and other condiments as well as dry and fresh ingredients. I would also highly recommend looking at online stores, as there are a number of excellent Irish-based international shops online that deliver anywhere in Ireland.

You might have heard the term 'cultural appropriation' being used recently – Jamie Oliver even has a consultant for such matters now – or read features about it in the media. The point is that cultural appropriation is about paying respect to where a recipe or dish comes from and giving credit to the origin of a dish. While there may be a lot of negativity around the topic, that is just

'He has taken something he loves from somewhere he loves and created his own unique version of it while giving credit to its origins.'

I think two of the cleverest uses of Korean flavours in this cookbook are in the toffee apple and doenjang caramel pudding (page 132) and the sweet potato and kimchi boxty (page 196). Boxty is quintessentially Irish, yet Graham has introduced foreign flavours in this perfect marriage of sweet potato and kimchi (spicy fermented cabbage), something that is quintessentially Korean. Fermentation is a trend that has really cemented itself in Irish food culture now after being lost for generations. Like Ireland, South Korea is a country that has a long history of colonisation, so its food identity was somewhat overshadowed by China's and Japan's for years. However, their innate fermentation techniques have created truly unique flavours that are easily identifiable as Korean. Kimchi is a prime example of this, but also doenjang, which is a fermented soybean paste.

because it's something we need to get right. Ireland is still in the early stages of our immigration journey and we can learn from the challenges that other countries have faced. We need to. Graham is a perfect example of how to do it correctly. His passion for flavours is his inspiration. He has taken something he loves from somewhere he loves and created his own unique version of it while giving credit to its origins.

The important thing is to embrace the flavours and cultures on our doorstep and bring the magic and variety of international cuisine to our tables at home. If in doubt, just follow Graham's lead. We all love the traditional, classic Irish recipes and they will always have their place in our hearts and kitchens, but Graham's skill at marrying the classics with his flair for flavour is what makes his recipes unique.

Baking

Baking powder and bread soda Baking powder and bread soda are both leavening agents, which means that they produce air bubbles in dough, causing it to rise. Bread soda must be mixed with a wet, acidic ingredient to activate it, such as the buttermilk in soda bread. Baking powder already has an acidic ingredient (usually cream of tartar) and only needs a liquid to activate it. Bread soda is also called bicarbonate of soda (or bicarb) or baking soda, but in this book I always refer to it as bread soda.

Butter I've used salted butter in all of the recipes in this book except for one (the radishes and butter on page 120), as I prefer the flavour. If you're using unsalted butter just add a pinch of salt, but if you're using salted butter, leave it out.

Buttercream frosting This is a simple frosting that's perfect for decorating the mammy buns on page 164 or for filling the Victoria sandwich on page 64. Using an electric hand mixer or a stand mixer fitted with the paddle attachment, start on a slow speed (or you'll have a big mess!) and beat 150g very soft butter with 300g icing sugar and 1 teaspoon of vanilla. Continue to beat for about 5 minutes, adding 1 or 2 tablespoons of milk if you would like to make the frosting a little softer.

Buttermilk Buttermilk is a fermented dairy product and traditionally it was the liquid left behind after churning butter – you will have some of your own if you make the butter on page 114. It's widely available in supermarkets but if you can't find it or if you need to make your own, simply add 1 tablespoon of lemon juice or white wine vinegar to every 250ml of milk required. Stir well and allow to stand at room temperature for 5–10 minutes to let it thicken before using.

Cooling Using a wire rack allows air to completely circulate around whatever is on it. Normally you allow your bake to cool in its tin for 5–10 minutes before transferring it to a wire rack to cool completely.

Creaming Creaming is the process of mixing softened butter and sugar into a light, fluffy, uniform and smooth mixture. The sugar should be dissolved and evenly mixed in. This is best done with an electric hand mixer or a stand mixer fitted with the paddle attachment but it can be done by hand using a wooden spoon.

Decorating cupcakes If you want to pipe the icing on a cupcake, my first tip is to start with a large open star nozzle. Next, make sure your buttercream frosting is very soft and spreadable. Start at the outside of the cupcake and work in a circular motion towards the centre on a slight angle to pipe the buttercream frosting around the cupcake. Don't hold the bag too close to the cupcake, as this gives you more control and stops the frosting being crushed. When you get to the centre, simply stop pushing the icing and pull away the piping bag. Alternatively, you can use a palette knife to decorate cupcakes. Simply use a back-and-forth motion to spread the frosting across the cupcake.

Dried fruit I've used dried fruit in a few recipes in this book. It normally refers to a mix of sultanas, raisins, currants and mixed peel. You can buy bags of pre-mixed dried fruit, but you can also use you own selection as long as the total weight is the same as that in the recipe. You could also try adding some dried apricots, dates or figs.

Dropping consistency What you are aiming for with a dropping consistency when making cakes is a cake batter that doesn't fall off the spoon easily, but rather, it reluctantly slides off the spoon after a few seconds.

Eggs All the recipes in this book use medium-sized free-range eggs. I store my eggs at room temperature since I use them quite quickly, but if you aren't going to use them as fast, store them in the fridge and take them out a few hours before you bake to let them come up to room temperature.

Folding In This is a method of incorporating light, airy mixtures like whisked eggs or cream with heavier components like flour or chocolate. The main aim is to keep as much air in the mixture as possible. This is done by either pouring the lighter mixture on top of the heavier one (mixing a light mixture with a heavy liquid) or gently sprinkling the heavy mixture on top of the light mixture (folding in flour) in a large bowl. Then, using a large metal spoon and starting at the back of the bowl, cut down through both mixtures. Lifting up at the side of the bowl that's closest to you, let any mixture you bring up gently fall into the centre of the bowl. Now rotate the bowl before repeating. Keep doing these light cuts, folds and rotations until both the mixtures are evenly combined.

Icing a cake First spread a small amount of the buttercream frosting on the bottom of a serving plate or cake board – this will help to secure the cake and stop it moving around. Place the first layer of sponge upside down on the plate so that the bottom of the sponge becomes the top. Using a palette knife, spread the required amount of buttercream frosting across the top of the sponge. Place the second sponge on top, again upside down. To stop crumbs from showing on your finished cake, apply a very thin coating of the frosting to the top and sides of the cake (in the trade, we call this a crumb coat) and chill in the fridge for 30 minutes, then finish your cake with a second coat of the frosting. For a rustic homemade look simply use the palette knife to make a rough finish, but if you would like a more refined finish, warm the palette knife in some hot water before using it to smooth the buttercream on your cake.

Measuring golden syrup, honey and treacle Either dip your measuring spoon into hot water or rub it with a drop of oil before measuring viscous things like golden syrup, honey or treacle. Also note that 1 tablespoon of these roughly weighs 20g.

Melting chocolate Chop the chocolate into small, even-sized pieces before adding it to a heatproof bowl set over a pan of gently simmering water. Make sure the chocolate doesn't come into contact with any water, which would cause the chocolate to seize and become unusable. You also need to make sure that the water doesn't touch the bottom of the bowl and that the water doesn't get too hot, as it may cause the chocolate to burn and split. Stir regularly for 4–5 minutes, until the chocolate is melted, and use as required. If you want to use a microwave, place the chocolate in a heatproof bowl, microwave it for 20 seconds, then stir. Continue microwaving for 10 seconds at a time and stirring each time until the chocolate is completely melted.

Oil I use vegetable oil in many recipes throughout this book, but feel free to use whichever type of oil you prefer, whether that's sunflower, rapeseed or olive oil. If you can find cold-pressed rapeseed oil, I suggest using it in the simple white loaf on page 40 as it adds the most amazing colour and flavour to the bread.

Oven temperatures Always preheat your oven. All the temperatures in the recipes in this book are based on a fan-assisted Celsius oven.

Rubbing in This is a method of combining flour and fat. Most of my recipes use butter, but it can refer to other fats like margarine. Cut the fat into small cubes before adding it to the flour. Using both hands, pick up the flour and fat and rub it lightly between your fingertips and thumb, lifting and rubbing above the bowl so that air can be incorporated. Continue until there is no loose flour or lumps of butter left and the mixture looks like fine breadcrumbs.

Salt Food needs salt. Adding it to a dish helps bring it to life by enhancing the flavour, as it is one of the five taste senses needed for the balance of a dish. Not only does it help to balance sweetness, but salt also helps to cut through richness. There are a few different types of salt available. Fine salt, like your standard table salt, is absolutely perfect for adding to recipes. Flaky sea salt (or finishing salt, as it's commonly called in the cheffing world) is perfect for finishing a dish, like the radishes on page 120 or even sprinkled on cookies (page 174) before you bake them. One of the most widely available flaky salts is Maldon, but there are now some amazing Irish flaky salt producers, such as Achill Sea Salt and Dingle Sea Salt Co. Coarse salt. The large crystals are perfect for using in a salt mill to grind into dishes using the same amount as fine salt.

Shortcrust pastry Shortcrust pastry is a French-style dough with a short, or crumbly, biscuit-like texture. This recipe is for a simple shortcrust pastry, used for the mushroom quiche on page 198 and the full Irish quiche on page 202. The sweet shortcrust or the enriched versions are perfect for the apple tart on page 134 and the gin, lemon and fuchsia tart on page 136. I sometimes like to bring my quiches to the next level by making them with a flavoured shortcrust.

200g plain flour
100g butter, chilled and diced
2–3 tbsp ice-cold water

Plain shortcrust pastry: Add the flour and butter to a food processor and pulse until it resembles fine breadcrumbs. Add 2 tablespoons of water and pulse again just until it starts to come together, adding a little more water if required. Use your hands to bring it together into a disc, then wrap it in cling film and chill in the fridge for about 30 minutes before using. If you don't have a food processor, you can use the rubbing-in method to make this pastry (see above).

Sweet shortcrust pastry: Add 25g icing sugar with the flour and butter.

Enriched shortcrust pastry: Use 1 egg yolk to replace 1 tablespoon of the water.

Flavoured shortcrust pastry: Add 1 teaspoon of dried herbs or dried mustard powder along with the flour and butter for an alternative base for a quiche. For an alternative sweet shortcrust, add the zest of a lemon or 1 teaspoon of vanilla extract.

Sifting Sifting ingredients such as flour and icing sugar removes any lumps and also helps to incorporate air, which all helps to achieve a lighter bake. Ingredients can also be sifted together to make processes easier, like sifting the flour and cocoa powder together for the brownie on page 158. This will make it a lot easier to fold in and get a smoother finish more quickly.

Sweet spice In lots of recipes throughout this book I have referred to sweet spice as an ingredient, which is just another name for mixed spice. I love to make my own sweet spice blend, but if you prefer, use shop-bought mixed spice. For my sweet spice blend I'm giving you the weight measurement as well as tablespoons and teaspoons because whole spices that you blend yourself have such a better flavour than pre-ground spices, so if you have a spice blender or coffee grinder, do try to use whole spices.

1 tbsp (8g) each of allspice, cinnamon and nutmeg

½ tbsp (4g) each of ground ginger, whole cloves, coriander seeds, fennel seeds and caraway seeds

¼ tsp (2g) green cardamom seeds (removed from their pods)

Simply grind and mix all the spices together and store them in a tightly sealed jar in a cool, dark place for up to 4 months.

Temperature of ingredients Unless otherwise stated, it's best to have all your ingredients at room temperature before you start baking, especially your eggs, butter and other dairy products. When at room temperature, these ingredients incorporate a lot more air when they are creamed or whipped, resulting in a lighter final bake.

Testing a cake or bread To test a cake: Insert a toothpick, thin-bladed knife or skewer into the centre of the bake. If it comes out clean, the bake is done. If it comes out sticky or with crumbs stuck to it, it's not done and needs more time in the oven. To test bread: Take the bread out of the oven, take it out of the tin (if using) and turn it over. Tap the bread on the bottom – bread should sound hollow when it's cooked. If it doesn't, it needs more time in the oven.

Tins I have limited the number of tins and dishes needed for the recipes in this book so that you don't need a massive selection. Here is what you'll need:

Loaf tin	900g (2lb)
Square baking tin	23cm (9in)
Square ceramic baking dish	23cm (9in)
Loose-bottomed tart tin	23cm (9in)
Cake tins x 2	20cm (8in)
Springform cake tin	20cm (8in)
Swiss roll tin/baking sheet	25cm (10in) x 38cm (15in)

When preparing a cake tin, simply rub the inside of the tin with a small amount of butter.

To line a circular tin: Cut a disc of non-stick baking paper to fit the bottom of your round tin. Use a long strip of the paper to go around the wall of the tin.

To line a square or loaf tin: Cut one rectangle that fits the bottom and up two sides, then repeat in the opposite direction.

To prepare a loaf tin for bread: Rub the inside of the tin with a little butter. Add 1 tablespoon of flour, then distribute the flour around the tin by tapping it gently. Tip out any excess flour.

Toasting nuts, seeds and spices Nuts: I find that the best way to toast nuts is to use the oven. Preheat the oven to 150°C fan. Place the nuts on a baking tray in a single loose layer and put in the oven. Every 5 minutes, take the tray out and move the nuts around to make sure they get an even colour. Depending on the type of nut, it may take anywhere between 10 and 20 minutes to toast evenly. **Seeds:** Add the seeds to a dry, heavy-based frying pan on a medium heat. Heat for 2–4 minutes, shaking the pan occasionally, until the seeds are golden brown and give off a nice toasted, nutty smell. **Spices:** I absolutely love using whole spices. Place the spices in a cold heavy-based frying pan, then put the pan on a medium heat and allow the spices to toast slowly, shaking the pan regularly to move the spices around. The spices will become very fragrant and start to brown – once this happens, immediately transfer them to a cool bowl and allow to cool completely before grinding in a spice mill or a clean coffee grinder.

Vanilla Vanilla is like butter – always use the best you can afford. When a recipe calls for vanilla, you have a few options. **Vanilla pod:** Whole vanilla pods are expensive, but if you like to use them, the seeds are simple to remove. Using a sharp knife, split the vanilla bean in half lengthways. Use the back of the knife to scrape the seeds out of the pod. But don't throw away the pod! Place it in a container of caster sugar to give the sugar a mild vanilla flavour and use it in other recipes. **Vanilla bean paste:** This is my preferred choice. It's a syrup made from vanilla extract and vanilla powder and has specks of vanilla beans suspended in it. **Vanilla extract:** This is a natural product that has a strong, deep flavour and stands up well to heat. To make your own vanilla extract, simply scrape the seeds out of five vanilla pods and add them to a small clean bottle or jam jar. Roughly chop up the pods and add them to the bottle or jar too. Top up with 125ml of clear alcohol, such as white rum or vodka, and shake well, then shake well every day. The extract will be ready to use after one week, but it keeps extremely well stored in a cool, dark place. **Vanilla essence:** This a synthetic product. Its flavour can be affected by the heat of cooking.

Whipping cream to soft or stiff peaks Pour your chilled cream into a large, cold bowl. Using an electric hand mixer or a stand mixer fitted with the whisk attachment and starting on a medium speed, start mixing the cream. Once you can see the cream start to thicken and leave a trail, you're almost there. Just a little bit more and you are at the soft peak stage, when the cream *just* about holds its shape. I love to serve it at this stage with things like apple tart and crumbles. Whip the cream a little more for stiff peaks – this is perfect for filling cakes or pavlovas. But if you go any further, the cream will start to split. If that happens, turn to page 114!

Whipping egg whites When whipping egg whites, make sure there is absolutely no egg yolk in with the egg whites, as any fat from the yolk will stop the whites from incorporating the air. You should also make sure your bowl and whisk are spotlessly clean and dry – I always wipe my bowl with a little white wine vinegar and some kitchen paper. Use an electric hand mixer or a stand mixer fitted with the whisk attachment for the best results. If adding sugar, add it slowly only after the eggs have reached a foamy stage or have doubled in volume.

~~~~~~

Umami Umami is one of the five basic tastes. It's a savoury taste – examples include eggs, cooked meat, mushrooms and air-dried tomatoes as well as things like Worcestershire sauce, ketchup and doenjang. Umami is a Japanese word that means 'essence of deliciousness', which in my opinion is beautiful. When you think about it, most bakes include a mild umami taste from the eggs.

~~~~~~

HOW TO READ A RECIPE

~~~~~~

If you're like me, you are currently curled up on the couch with a big mug of tea reading this book like a novel or tucked up in bed enjoying a few pages. On the other hand, if you are standing in the kitchen about to start baking something from this book – or indeed, any cookbook – there are a couple of things you need to do so that you don't get caught out. Trust me, I'm talking from bitter experience here!

- Before you do anything else, read the recipe carefully and all the way to the end so that there are no surprises halfway through baking.

- Double check that you have all the ingredients and enough of each. The same goes for tins, dishes and bowls – do you have the right size?

- I know it might seem like a pain to have all your ingredients weighed out in advance, but it really is worth the effort and makes the actual baking or cooking of the dish so much more enjoyable.

EVERYTHING YOU NEED TO KNOW BUT WERE AFRAID TO ASK ABOUT

Ingredients

I have used some ingredients in this book that you may not have come across before. To be honest, it annoys me when a recipe calls for an ingredient that's hard to find and it can put me off making a recipe. Plus what do you do with the open jar or packet after you've made the recipe? Hopefully this little guide will help you out. If you don't have something or can't find it locally, I have suggested an alternative. For those open packets and jars, I have suggested alternative uses.

ADVIEH What is it? A spice blend used in savoury Persian dishes such as stews, soups, grilled meats and rice pilaf. It consists of dried rose petals, cardamom seeds, cumin seeds, ground cinnamon and ground ginger. **Where can I buy it?** Most Middle Eastern stores and Indian specialty shops. **What can I use instead?** I can't recommend this blend highly enough, but if you can't source it, make you own blend with the spices listed in the recipe intro for sholeh zard on page 154. **What else can I use it for?** It makes an amazing rub for meats and is a great seasoning for rice.

BLACK SESAME SEEDS What is it? The dried fruit pods of the sesame plant. **Where can I buy it?** Asian supermarkets. **What can I use instead?** White sesame seeds. **What else can I use it for?** Use in the same way as white sesame seeds.

CHINESE FIVE-SPICE POWDER What is it? A blend of five or more spices used in a lot of Chinese cooking as well as the cuisines of Hawaii and

Vietnam. **Where can I buy it?** Local supermarkets. **What can I use instead?** A mix of garam masala and star anise. **What else can I use it for?** I love it on roast vegetables and in a stir-fry.

CONFIT DUCK LEGS (CONFIT DE CANARD) What is it? Duck legs slowly cooked in duck fat until tender. **Where can I buy it?** Most supermarkets and specialist food stores sell confit duck legs, such as the Irish brand Silver Hill. Sheridans Cheesemongers also have one under their own brand. **What can I use instead?** A duck breast, cooked and cooled before using. **What else can I use it for?** Delicious with a crisp salad served with orange segments or with slow-cooked Puy lentils.

DOENJANG What is it? A Korean fermented soybean paste that has a slightly funky taste. **Where can I buy it?** Asian supermarkets. **What can I use instead?** Miso paste. **What else can I use it for?** Use in a similar way to miso.

HOISIN What is it? A fragrant sauce used in Cantonese cuisine. **Where can I buy it?** Local supermarkets. **What can I use instead?** Teriyaki sauce. **What else can I use it for?** Great with duck pancakes or in stir-fries.

KEWPIE MAYONNAISE What is it? An egg yolk mayonnaise from Japan. **Where can I buy it?** Asian supermarkets. **What can I use instead?** Regular mayo with a dash of rice wine vinegar. **What else can I use it for?** Use it the same way as regular mayo – I love it on chicken sandwiches.

KIMCHI What is it? A Korean dish of fermented vegetables, usually napa cabbage. **Where can I buy it?** Asian shops and health food stores. **What can I use instead?** Sauerkraut mixed with a little chilli. **What else can I use it for?** Delicious in a cheese toastie, also great with eggs.

MAHLEB What is it? A spice made from the seed of the mahleb or St Lucie cherry stone. **Where can I buy it?** Middle Eastern stores. **What can I use instead?** Almond extract with a little star anise; kirsch. **What else can I use it for?** Adds great depth of flavour anywhere that you would use almonds or cherries.

MATCHA POWDER What is it? Fine powder made from specialty green tea leaves. **Where can I buy it?** Asian shops (and most large supermarkets will also have a version). **What can I use instead?** Unfortunately, there really aren't any substitutes for this unique flavour. **What else can I use it for?** Makes an amazing hot drink.

MISO PASTE What is it? A Japanese fermented soybean paste made using salt and koji. **Where can I buy it?** Asian supermarkets and most large supermarkets stock it. **What can I use instead?** Doenjang or a dash of soy sauce can add that salty, savoury flavour. **What else can I use it for?** Make your own miso soup. It's fantastic mixed with butter for miso butter and it also adds a great umami note to soups and stews.

PANCH PHORON What is it? A whole spice mix containing cumin, brown mustard, fennel, nigella and fenugreek that is used in the cuisines of Eastern India and Bangladesh. **Where can I buy it?** Most Middle Eastern stores and Indian specialty shops. **What can I use instead?** Mustard seeds on their own or ideally mixed with some celery seeds. **What else can I use it for?** Use it in homemade chutneys or to season vegetables and meats.

POMEGRANATE MOLASSES What is it? A seasoning made from concentrated pomegranate juice. **Where can I buy it?** Turkish shops and Asian supermarkets. **What can I use instead?** Honey with a squeeze of lemon juice. **What else can I use it for?** Use as a cordial and top up with sparkling water for a refreshing cool drink.

TAHINI PASTE What is it? A Middle Eastern condiment made from ground roast sesame seeds. **Where can I buy it?** Turkish shops and most supermarkets. **What can I use instead?** Cashew or almond butter. **What else can I use it for?** As a dip for raw vegetables, on toast or with falafel.

Bread

&

Scones

Brown soda bread

As we begin our journey in Irish baking, it's only proper that we start with brown soda bread. There is something about the smell of freshly baked brown bread that triggers so many emotional connections for me – to a person, Mrs Supple, and the giant loaves I remember from my childhood; to a place, when myself and my husband, Daithí, ate seafood chowder and brown bread in Doolin; and to a time, when on a recent visit to my brother and his family, his wife had just baked brown bread and the smell filled their house with a warm, welcoming aroma. I truly believe that making a loaf of bread is more than just an action – it's an invitation to the people you are going to share it with, a symbol of generosity and a gesture of love.

Makes 1 x 900g (2lb) loaf

melted butter, for greasing

250g wholemeal flour, plus a little extra for dusting the top

200g plain flour, plus extra for dusting the tin

1 tsp bread soda

1 tsp salt

400ml buttermilk

2 tbsp vegetable oil

1 tsp honey

Preheat the oven to 180°C fan. Prepare a 900g (2lb) loaf tin by lightly brushing it with melted butter and dusting with a little plain flour.

Place all the dry ingredients in a large bowl and gently mix.

In a separate jug, gently whisk all the wet ingredients together with a fork, then mix this into the dry ingredients. Add a little more buttermilk if the mixture is too dry – it should be a soft, wet dough.

Pour the dough into the prepared tin and sprinkle a little extra wholemeal flour on top. Bake in the preheated oven for 45–50 minutes. To check it's baked, remove the bread from the tin and tap the bottom – it should sound hollow when it's fully cooked. If it doesn't, keep the bread out of the tin and put it back in the oven directly on the oven rack for an extra 5 minutes and check it again.

Remove from the oven and wrap in a clean tea towel while it's cooling – this will stop the crust getting too hard.

WITH A
Twist

With a little imagination, you can make your brown soda loaf very special. Think about what you want to serve the bread with, as that may provide some inspiration – maybe add some rosemary and use the bread as an accompaniment to a lamb stew or add a tablespoon of wholegrain mustard and use the bread for a ham sandwich. These variations are for the brown soda bread on page 22.

SEEDED

Add 50g mixed seeds with the dry ingredients and sprinkle some extra seeds on top before baking. Packets of seed mixes are widely available and usually contain a mix of pumpkin, sunflower, sesame and flax seeds. Keep an eye out for hemp seeds, which have an amazing nutty taste. You can also make your own mix of seeds or just use your favourite one or two.

SUN-DRIED TOMATO & BASIL

Add 75g finely chopped sun-dried tomatoes and a small handful of shredded fresh basil leaves (or if you are a fan of basil, you can always add more!) just before you add the liquid. And don't let the oil from the jar of sun-dried tomatoes go to waste – use it to replace the vegetable oil in the original recipe and to boost the flavour.

DILL & LEMON

Add three or four chopped sprigs of fresh dill and the zest of one lemon just before you add the liquids. Some poppy seeds sprinkled on top really add to this version too, which is delicious with smoked fish or soft goats' cheese.

WALNUT & FIG

Add 50g chopped walnuts and 50g finely chopped dried figs with the dry ingredients and add an additional teaspoon of honey to the wet ingredients. Sprinkle some extra chopped walnuts on top before putting in the oven. This bread is great with cheese, especially blue cheese.

Guinness brown bread

Guinness brown bread has become iconic over the years. My favourite way to eat it is sliced and topped with some horseradish crème fraîche, smoked salmon and pickled red onion, all accompanied by a glass of the black stuff!

Makes 1 x 900g (2lb) loaf

melted butter, for greasing the tin

300g coarse wholemeal flour

150g plain flour, plus extra for dusting the tin

50g porridge oats, plus extra to sprinkle on top

1 tsp bread soda

1 tsp salt

250ml buttermilk

200ml Guinness stout

100g treacle

2 tbsp vegetable oil

To serve:

smoked salmon

horseradish crème fraîche (see the note)

pickled red onion (see the note)

chopped fresh chives

Preheat the oven to 180°C fan. Prepare a 900g (2lb) loaf tin by lightly brushing it with melted butter and dusting with a little plain flour.

Place all the dry ingredients in a large bowl and gently mix.

In a separate jug, gently whisk all the wet ingredients together with a fork, then mix this into the dry ingredients. Add a little more buttermilk if the mixture is too dry – it should be a soft, wet dough.

Pour the dough into the prepared tin and sprinkle some extra porridge oats on top. Bake in the preheated oven for 55 minutes. Carefully take the bread out of the tin and place it back in the oven on the rack for a further 5 minutes. To check if the bread is baked, tap the bottom – it should sound hollow when fully cooked.

Remove from the oven and wrap in a clean tea towel while it's cooling to stop the crust getting too hard. Serve with smoked salmon, horseradish crème fraîche and pickled red onion and garnish with chopped fresh chives.

Note

To make the horseradish crème fraîche, simply stir a teaspoon of horseradish sauce into a small tub of crème fraîche. For the pickled red onion, halve and thinly slice a red onion. Pour over 4 tablespoons white wine vinegar, 1 teaspoon salt and 1 teaspoon caster sugar. Leave to stand for 1 hour before using.

Rye, ale & honey bread

I wanted to create a bread that worked really well with baked ham and cold meats. My dad was a pork butcher, so it's only natural that he is the inspiration for this recipe. He loves a pint of Smithwick's and with a surname like Herterich, I had to look to Germany for some inspiration. I've used rye flour and lots of seeds, like so many good German breads. I love this bread served with the honey and mustard baked ham on page 206 along with some good salted butter, gherkins and mustard. Pass the Kölsch – *prost*!

Makes 1 x 900g (2lb) loaf

melted butter, for greasing the tin

300g dark rye flour

150g plain flour, plus extra for dusting the tin

100g pumpkin seeds, plus extra to sprinkle on top

1 tsp bread soda

1 tsp salt

250ml buttermilk

250ml ale

75g honey

2 tbsp vegetable oil

Preheat the oven to 180°C fan. Prepare a 900g (2lb) loaf tin by lightly brushing it with melted butter and dusting with a little plain flour.

Place all the dry ingredients in a large bowl and gently mix.

In a separate jug, whisk all the wet ingredients together with a fork, then mix this into the dry ingredients.

Pour the dough into the prepared tin and sprinkle some porridge oats on top. Bake in the preheated oven for 1 hour, then take the bread out of the tin and place it back in the oven, straight on the oven rack, for a further 5 minutes. To check it's baked, tap the bottom of the bread – it should sound hollow when it's fully cooked.

Remove from the oven and wrap in a clean tea towel while it's cooling to stop the crust getting too hard.

White soda bread
with guggy in a cup

As I've been researching and writing this book, I've been thinking back to different childhood memories and trying to remember who, where and when my different food loves come from. My love of butter is definitely due to my Granny Daisy. If we were staying in her house for tea, chances are we would get guggy in a cup served with buttery toast. The term 'guggy' comes from a child's name for an egg in the Irish language, *gug* or *gugaí*. Guggy is simply a soft-boiled egg, mashed and served in a cup. In Granny Daisy's house, the toast was only ever cooked under the gas grill, on one side only, and topped with a decadent layer of golden buttery goodness. The guggy was served in a willow pattern cup and always contained a good knob of butter. Granny Daisy really did make the most delicious guggy and I think my recipe for a traditional white Irish soda bread is the perfect accompaniment for it.

Makes 1 x 900g (2lb) loaf; guggy serves 1

melted butter, for greasing the tin

450g plain flour, plus extra for dusting the tin and to sprinkle on top

1 tsp bread soda

1 tsp salt

400ml buttermilk

1 medium egg, beaten

2 tbsp vegetable oil

Preheat the oven to 180°C fan. Prepare your 900g (2lb) loaf tin by lightly brushing it with melted butter and dusting with a little plain flour.

Place all the dry ingredients in a large bowl and gently mix.

In a separate jug, whisk the buttermilk, egg and oil together with a fork, then mix this into the dry ingredients. Add a little more buttermilk if the mixture is too dry – it should be a soft dough.

Pour the dough into the prepared tin and sprinkle a light dusting of flour on top. Bake in the preheated oven for 45–50 minutes. To check it's cooked, take the bread out of the tin and tap the bottom – it should sound hollow when fully cooked.

Remove from the oven and wrap in a clean tea towel while it's cooling to stop the crust getting too hard.

For the guggy egg in a cup:

2 medium eggs

1 tsp butter

salt and pepper to taste

To make the guggy egg in a cup, soft boil the eggs. My favourite way to soft boil eggs is to slowly lower them into a pan of boiling water, reduce to a simmer and cook for 5–6 minutes.

Mash the eggs in a pre-warmed teacup with the butter and season to taste. Enjoy with thick slices of the toasted soda bread and by all means toast the bread on both sides if you feel like it – I'm sure Granny Daisy wouldn't be offended.

Panch phoron soda bread
with lamb keema curry

Panch phoron, which translates as five spice, is a whole spice mix containing cumin, brown mustard, fennel, nigella and fenugreek. It's popular in the cuisines of Eastern India and Bangladesh and has a robust yet aromatic flavour. I love to serve this bread cut into slices and toasted on a ridged chargrill pan or griddle, served with the lamb keema curry, some yogurt and fresh coriander. The combination of this bread and the curry is a hat tip to the amazing goat keema pao made by Sunil Ghai of Pickle restaurant in Dublin. It's one of Sunil's signature dishes – your first memory of eating it will stay with you forever.

Makes 1 x 20cm round loaf; curry serves 4

For the panch phoron soda bread:

4 tbsp vegetable oil

1 medium onion, halved and thinly sliced

3 garlic cloves, finely chopped

2 tbsp panch phoron, plus a little extra to sprinkle on top

1 tbsp ground turmeric

500g plain flour, plus extra for dusting

1 tsp bread soda

a small bunch of fresh coriander, leaves and stalks finely chopped

1 tsp salt

a pinch of freshly ground black pepper

350ml buttermilk

1 medium egg, beaten

To make the bread, heat the oil in a frying pan on a medium heat. Add the onion and cook for about 10 minutes, stirring occasionally, until the onion is golden. Add the garlic, panch phoron and turmeric and cook for another 2–3 minutes to allow the spices to release their flavour. Take the pan off the heat and allow to cool.

Preheat the oven to 180°C fan. Prepare a baking sheet by lightly dusting it with a little plain flour.

Place the flour and bread soda in a large bowl and mix well using a table knife. Make a well in the centre of the flour, then add the cooled spiced onion, chopped fresh coriander, salt, pepper and the buttermilk. Mix gently before starting to incorporate them into the flour using a table knife. Bring the dough together, then tip it out onto a lightly floured surface and gently knead and shape the dough into a 20cm round.

Put the bread on the baking sheet and cut a deep cross on the top, then brush with the beaten egg - try not to get any egg into the cut lines - and sprinkle with a little more panch phoron. Bake in the preheated oven for 45 minutes, then turn the bread upside down and cook for a further 10 minutes. To check if the bread is baked, tap the bottom - it should sound hollow when fully cooked. Wrap in a clean tea towel while it's cooling to stop the crust getting too hard. ⊕

For the lamb keema curry:

2 tbsp vegetable oil

1 medium onion, halved and thinly sliced

3 garlic cloves, finely chopped

2 fresh red chillies, deseeded and finely chopped

a thumb-sized piece of fresh ginger, peeled and grated

500g minced lamb

2 tbsp panch phoron

2 tbsp curry powder (mild or hot – your choice)

1 tbsp ground turmeric

1 x 400g tin of chopped tomatoes

200g frozen peas

2 tbsp natural yogurt

a small bunch of fresh coriander, leaves and stalks finely chopped

To make the curry, heat the oil in a frying pan over a medium heat. Add the onion and cook for 8 minutes before adding the garlic, chillies and ginger. Cook for another 2 minutes, until everything has softened.

Turn up the heat to high before adding the lamb and breaking it up gently with a spoon. Cook for about 10 minutes but try not to overmix or move the lamb too much at this stage, allowing it to get a nice fried colour before moving it around again.

Add the spices and cook for a further 2–3 minutes, then add the tinned tomatoes and half a tin of water and bring to the boil. Reduce the heat and simmer for 20 minutes.

Add the frozen peas and yogurt and simmer for another 10 minutes. Stir in the coriander just before serving with toasted slices of the panch phoron soda bread.

Curnie cake

Curnie cake conjures up childhood memories of Sunday drives to visit my grand-aunt, Mrs Tobin, and her husband, Uncle Mick, on their dairy farm in Kilbride, County Carlow. She was an amazing baker and had a huge Aga in her kitchen where she would make soda breads, apple tarts, coffee cake and of course curnie cake. With all the baked goodies and the fresh-from-the-cow milk taken straight from the churn, it's no wonder I have great memories of our visits there.

This bake seems to have lots of regional names (fruit soda bread, spotted dog or railway cake) and lots of people have their own name for it, like nanny bread, or it's even named after the person who made it, like Mrs O'Donnell Bread. But to me, it will always be curnie cake.

Serves 8

450g plain flour

25g caster sugar, plus extra for sprinkling on top

1 tsp salt

1 tsp bread soda

25g butter, chilled and diced

100g dried fruit (raisins, sultanas, currants or a mix)

350ml buttermilk

1 medium egg, beaten

Preheat the oven to 180°C fan. Prepare a baking sheet by lightly dusting it with a little plain flour.

Place the dry ingredients in a large bowl and mix well. Add the butter and rub it together with your fingertips until the mixture looks like fine breadcrumbs. Gently mix in the dried fruit.

Add the buttermilk and use a table knife to mix together to form a rough dough, then use your hands to gently bring the dough together and shape into a 20cm round.

Put the loaf on the baking sheet and cut a deep cross on the top. Brush the top with the beaten egg, but try not to get any into the cut lines.

Bake in the preheated oven for 45 minutes, then turn the bread upside down and cook for a further 10 minutes. To check it's baked, tap the bottom of the bread – it should sound hollow when fully cooked. Wrap in a clean tea towel while it's cooling to stop the crust getting too hard.

Variations

CURRENT
(not currant!)
CAKE

The previous recipe for curnie cake gets its name (I think!) from the currants that would have traditionally been in it. But as I said above, it has lots of names, so I could be wrong. I'm dyslexic and when I was writing that last recipe, I spelled currant wrong EVERY. SINGLE. TIME. I spelled it as current, so I'm taking this opportunity to make currant cake current! Here are some of my ideas for modern twists that simply replace the dried fruit in the previous recipe.

APRICOT, ALMOND & DARK CHOCOLATE

Add 20g cocoa powder to the dry ingredients. Replace the dried fruit with 75g sliced dried apricots, 75g dark chocolate chips and 20g flaked almonds. Add ½ teaspoon almond extract to the wet ingredients and sprinkle some extra flaked almonds on top before baking.

CHEDDAR & MARMALADE

The sweet bitterness of marmalade is such a good contrast to a strong mature Cheddar cheese. Leave out the sugar from the currant cake recipe, then add 80g grated mature Cheddar and the zest of 1 orange before adding the wet ingredients. Stir 2 large tablespoons of marmalade into the wet ingredients before adding them to the dry.

ROAST SQUASH & MAPLE SYRUP

Peel a butternut squash and cut it into 2cm dice. Place in a bowl and sprinkle with 2 tablespoons maple syrup and 1 teaspoon sweet spice (page 15) or mixed spice, tossing to coat. Place the squash on a baking tray lined with non-stick baking paper and roast in a hot oven (200°C) for 15 minutes. Allow to cool before adding to the dry ingredients just before you add the buttermilk. Sprinkle some pumpkin seeds on top of the bread just before baking.

GREEN OLIVE, WHITE CHOCOLATE & LEMON

I know this combination sounds completely out there, but think about it – you often see dark chocolate and sea salt paired together. In that same vein, the slightly savoury, salty taste of the olives works so well with the sweet floral notes of the white chocolate.

Don't use the butter in the original currie cake recipe and instead add 25ml olive oil with the wet ingredients. Use 75g sliced green olives, 75g white chocolate chips and the zest of 1 lemon instead of the dried fruit.

Simple white loaf

I love a slice of brack and butter, but bread and butter is a very close second, especially when the bread is freshly cooked, light and fluffy. I have written already in the brown soda bread recipe on page 22 that I think baking soda bread is more about sharing and is quite wholesome. Making white bread, on the other hand, is definitely personal. Only you will know the frustrations and stresses that can be released while kneading, and for a few brief seconds when you open the oven door, you can bask in the sight and aroma knowing that you have made that loaf of bread and that the steam is your frustrations evaporating!

Makes 1 x 900g (2lb) loaf

500g strong white flour, plus extra for dusting

1 x 7g sachet of fast-action dried yeast

1 tbsp caster sugar

1 tsp salt

300ml warm water

25ml cold-pressed rapeseed oil, plus extra for greasing

Using a stand mixer fitted with the dough hook, combine all the ingredients on a slow speed before increasing the speed and kneading for 8–10 minutes, until it has come together into a smooth dough.

Or if you like to work for your food, combine the flour, yeast, sugar and salt in a large bowl. Slowly add the water and oil, continuing to mix using your hands until you have a soft dough. Tip the dough out onto a lightly greased surface (see the note overleaf) and knead by hand for 10–12 minutes, until the dough is smooth and elastic. To knead dough by hand, fold it in half and push it forward using the heel of your hand to press the dough flat. Turn the dough by a quarter, fold it in half and repeat. Keep doing this for as long as the recipe states – in this case, 10–12 minutes (sorry!).

Put the dough in a large, lightly greased bowl and either place the entire bowl in a large clean plastic bag or cover it with cling film. Place in a warm, draught-free place for about 1 hour, until the dough has doubled in size.

While the dough is proving, prepare a 900g (2lb) loaf tin by lightly greasing it and dusting with flour.

Punch the dough down and knead it again for 5 minutes. Shape into a log that will fit your loaf tin before placing it in the prepared tin. Cover loosely again and leave to rise for another 30 minutes.

Preheat the oven to 200°C fan. ➔

Uncover the bread and using a sharp knife, score a line lengthways down the middle. Put the bread in the preheated oven and immediately reduce the temperature to 180°C fan. Bake for 30–35 minutes. I like to throw a few ice cubes into the bottom of the oven at this stage to create some steam, which helps the bread to rise.

Remove the bread from the tin and check that it's baked by tapping the bottom of the loaf – it should sound hollow when it's fully cooked. If it doesn't, put it back in the oven for a few more minutes.

Allow to cool on a wire rack for at least 30 minutes before slicing – it's worth the wait.

Note

I prefer to knead yeast breads on a lightly greased surface as I find that it prevents the dough drying out. This works perfectly well on marble, stainless steel and laminated worktops. To grease the surface, spread a tablespoon of vegetable oil on the area you will be using to knead. If you want to dust your work surface with flour, though, try to use as little as possible.

Miso & sesame loaf

One of my favourite breads ever is the miso and sesame sourdough made by Scéal Bakery in Dublin. If you get a chance to try it, do – you won't regret it. The flavour is stunning, with the umami from the miso and the toasted nuttiness of the sesame. I've taken inspiration from Scéal's combination for this elevated simple white loaf.

Makes 1 x 900g (2lb) loaf

500g strong white flour, plus extra for dusting

25g sesame seeds, plus extra to coat the bread

1 x 7g sachet of fast-action dried yeast

1 tbsp caster sugar

1 tsp salt

300ml warm water

25ml sesame oil, plus extra for greasing

25g miso paste

Using a stand mixer fitted with the dough hook, combine all the ingredients on a slow speed before increasing the speed and kneading for 8–10 minutes, until it has come together into a smooth dough.

Or if you like to work for your food, combine the flour, sesame seeds, yeast, sugar and salt in a large bowl. Use a fork to whisk the water, oil and miso together in a jug, then slowly add this to the dry ingredients, continuing to mix until you have a soft dough.

Tip the dough out onto a lightly greased surface (see the note overleaf) and knead by hand for 10–12 minutes, until the dough is smooth and elastic. To knead dough by hand, fold it in half and push it forward using the heel of your hand to press the dough flat. Turn the dough by a quarter, fold it in half and repeat. Keep doing this for as long as the recipe states – in this case, 10–12 minutes (sorry!).

Put the dough in a large, lightly greased bowl and either place the entire bowl in a large clean plastic bag or cover it with cling film. Place in a warm, draught-free place for about 1 hour, until the dough has doubled in size.

While the dough is proving, prepare a 900g (2lb) loaf tin by lightly greasing it and dusting with flour.

Punch the dough down and knead it again for 5 minutes. Shape into a log that will fit your loaf tin before rolling the entire log in extra sesame seeds and placing it in the prepared tin. Cover loosely again and leave to rise for another 30 minutes.

Preheat the oven to 200°C fan. ⊕

Uncover the bread and using a sharp knife, score a line lengthways down the middle of the bread. Put the bread in the preheated oven and immediately reduce the temperature to 180°C fan. Bake for 30–35 minutes. I like to throw a few ice cubes into the bottom of the oven at this stage to create some steam, which helps the bread to rise.

Remove the bread from the tin and check that it's baked by tapping the bottom of the loaf – it should sound hollow when it's fully cooked. If it doesn't, put it back in the oven for a few more minutes.

Allow to cool on a wire rack for at least 30 minutes before slicing – it's worth the wait.

Note

I prefer to knead yeast breads on a
lightly greased surface as I find that it
prevents the dough drying out. This
works perfectly well on marble, stainless
steel and laminated worktops. To grease
the surface, spread a tablespoon of
vegetable oil on the area you will be
using to knead. If you want to dust your
work surface with flour, though, try to
use as little as possible.

Iced duck

The term 'iced duck' was new to me when I started working on this book, but the concept of an iced fruit loaf wasn't. An iced loaf is basically a bread enriched with butter and milk, with dried fruit and spices added in and topped with a sugary glaze. I remember getting it from Bradbury's, our local bakery in Athy, when I was growing up.

Makes 1 large loaf

400g strong white flour, plus extra for dusting

40g light brown sugar

40g butter, softened, plus extra for greasing

10g fast-action dried yeast

1 tsp salt

120ml milk, warmed slightly

120ml water, warmed slightly

60g dried mixed fruit

50g glacé cherries

1 tsp sweet spice (page 15) or mixed spice

zest and juice of 1 orange (use the juice for the icing)

zest of 1 lemon

200g icing sugar

Combine the flour, brown sugar, butter, yeast and salt in the bowl of a stand mixer fitted with the dough hook. Slowly add the milk and water, mixing until you have a soft dough. Knead for about 10 minutes, until the dough is smooth and feels stretchy. Or you can mix and knead the dough by hand – see the instructions in the simple white loaf on page 40.

Place the dough in a large greased bowl and either put the entire bowl into a large clean plastic bag or cover it with cling film and allow to rise in a warm, draught-free place for about 1 hour, until it has doubled in size.

Prepare a large baking tray by greasing it with butter and dusting it with some flour.

Punch down the dough, then add the dried fruit, cherries, spice and orange and lemon zest to the bowl. Work these into the dough using your hands.

Using a rolling pin, roll out the dough into a large oval shape roughly 26cm x 23cm, then roll it up widthways into a long sausage, like you would for making a Swiss roll. Place on the prepared baking tray, seam side down, cover loosely again and leave to rise for another 45 minutes.

Preheat the oven to 200°C fan.

Bake the loaf in the preheated oven for 25–30 minutes, until it's golden brown and sounds hollow when tapped on the bottom. Allow to cool on a wire rack.

While the loaf is cooling, make the icing by gradually mixing the orange juice with the icing sugar just until its consistency coats the back of a spoon. Drizzle the icing over the cooled loaf and enjoy sliced with a little butter.

Lucky duck

As I was researching the bread for this book I kept referring to iced duck as 'lucky duck', hence the recipe I developed for the modern version of an iced duck. I knew I wanted to create something savoury and I knew that I wanted it to include duck. What I eventually conjured up is this enriched loaf flavoured with confit duck, spring onions, Chinese five-spice and hoisin sauce, served with a duck butter and a refreshing smashed cucumber salad. My suggestion is that you serve everything together as a sharing dish.

Makes 1 large loaf

400g strong white flour, plus extra for dusting

40g butter, plus extra for greasing

10g fast-action dried yeast

1 tbsp caster sugar

1 tsp salt

1 tsp Chinese five-spice powder

120ml milk, warmed slightly

120ml water, warmed slightly

2 confit duck legs

30g spring onions, finely chopped

2 tbsp hoisin sauce, plus extra for serving

Combine the flour, butter, yeast, sugar, salt and five-spice powder in the bowl of a stand mixer fitted with the dough hook. Slowly add the milk and water, mixing until you have a soft dough. Knead for about 10 minutes, until the dough is smooth and feels stretchy. Or you can mix and knead the dough by hand – see the instructions in the simple white loaf on page 40.

Place the dough in a large greased bowl and either put the entire bowl into a large clean plastic bag or cover it with cling film and allow to rise in a warm, draught-free place for about 1 hour, until it has doubled in size.

Prepare a large baking tray by greasing it with butter and dusting it with some flour. Pick the duck meat off the bones and finely chop it. Reserve the skin for the duck butter.

Punch down the dough, then add half of the duck and all of the spring onions (you'll use the rest of the duck in the duck butter). Work these into the dough using your hands.

Using a rolling pin, roll out the dough into a large oval shape roughly 26cm x 23cm, then brush with the hoisin sauce and roll it up widthways into a long sausage, like you would for making a Swiss roll. Place on the prepared baking tray, seam side down, cover loosely again and leave to rise for another 45 minutes.

Preheat the oven to 200°C fan.

Bake the loaf in the preheated oven for 25–30 minutes, until it's golden brown and sounds hollow when tapped on the bottom. Allow to cool on a wire rack. ➔

For the duck butter:

reserved duck skin and chopped meat

300g butter, softened

¼ tsp Chinese five-spice powder

For the smashed cucumber salad:

2 cucumbers

1 tbsp rice wine vinegar

1 tbsp sesame oil

1 tbsp chilli oil

1 tbsp soy sauce

½ tsp salt

2 garlic cloves, finely chopped

1 fresh red chilli, deseeded and thinly sliced

a small handful of fresh coriander, finely · chopped

2 tsp toasted sesame seeds

Meanwhile, to make the duck butter, finely cut the duck skin into thin slices and add to a cold frying pan (starting in a cold pan allows the fat to render out of the skin). Turn the heat up to high and fry until crisp, then add the rest of the duck meat and fry for another minute.

Using a sieve, separate the skin and meat from the fat and reserve the fat. Allow both to cool.

Mix the softened butter with the cooled duck fat and the five-spice powder. Once combined, gently stir in the duck meat and skin. Shape the butter into a log and roll in non-stick baking paper, twisting the ends. Refrigerate to firm it up. Take the butter out of the fridge about half an hour before serving.

To make the salad, use a rolling pin to smash the cucumbers until they split, then cut them into bite-sized pieces. Whisk together the rice wine vinegar, sesame oil, chilli oil, soy sauce and salt. Place the cucumbers in a large bowl with the garlic, chilli, coriander and toasted sesame seeds, then pour over the wet ingredients. Allow to infuse for about 10 minutes before serving.

Serve the bread, duck butter and smashed cucumber salad together, sharing style, with extra hoisin on the side.

Plain scones

I love going to a fancy hotel for afternoon tea, but to be honest, my favourite part is the savoury bits – followed extremely closely by the warm, buttery scones. I don't care which goes on a scone first, jam or cream, as long as there are lots of toppings to adorn these little beauties.

Makes 8

350g self-raising flour, plus extra for dusting

45g caster sugar

1 tsp baking powder

85g cold butter, cut into small pieces

1 tsp vanilla (optional)

zest of ½ lemon (optional)

180ml buttermilk

1 medium egg, beaten

Preheat the oven to 200°C fan. Line a baking sheet with non-stick baking paper.

Place the flour, sugar and baking powder in a large bowl and mix well using your fingers. Add the butter and rub together until the mixture looks like fine breadcrumbs.

Add the vanilla and lemon zest (if desired), then stir in the buttermilk and mix everything together using a table knife to form a soft dough.

Turn out onto a lightly floured surface. Lightly flour the top of the dough and gently bring it together. Using a rolling pin, roll out the dough to a thickness of 3cm. Use a 6cm round cutter to stamp out the scones. Lightly knead the trimmings together and roll and cut like before.

Place the scones on the lined baking sheet and brush the tops with the beaten egg. Bake in the preheated oven for 12–14 minutes, until they are nicely risen and golden brown.

Variations

A BRILLIANCE OF SCONES

Animals have the most amazing collective nouns, like a flamboyance of flamingos, a pride of lions, a parliament of owls or even an unkindness of ravens! Unfortunately for food, the collective nouns are not as fabulous – a bag of flour, a carton of eggs or in this case, a batch of scones. These scones deserve a better name than that, so from this day forth I'm going to call a batch of fancy scones *a brilliance of scones* because that is what they are – brilliant! For each of these versions, use the plain scone recipe on page 54 as the starting point.

FRUIT

After adding the butter, leave out the vanilla and lemon zest and add 100g dried fruit of your choice, such as sultanas, raisins, glacé cherries and/or mixed peel, 1 teaspoon sweet spice mix (page 15) or mixed spice and the zest of a mandarin or clementine. Fruit scones may take slightly longer to cook.

RASPBERRY & WHITE CHOCOLATE

Add 75g frozen raspberries and 50g white chocolate chips just before you add the buttermilk. I like to use frozen berries as they tend to hold together and don't break up as much. These scones will need an extra 5 minutes of baking time in the oven because of the frozen fruit.

BANANA, CHOCOLATE & HAZELNUT

Most baking recipes that use bananas will call for them to be overripe or even black, but in this recipe I prefer to use slightly underripe ones as they hold together better and you get little pieces in your scone.

Add 20g cocoa powder to the dry ingredients as you work in the butter. Then, just before you add the buttermilk, add 1 finely diced underripe banana, 50g milk chocolate chips and 50g roughly chopped, toasted hazelnuts. These scones are great topped with chocolate hazelnut spread.

BLUEBERRY & ALMOND

Add 75g fresh blueberries, cut in half, and 50g flaked almonds to the dry ingredients. Add ½ teaspoon almond essence to the buttermilk. Sprinkle some extra flaked almonds on top of the scones after you brush them with the beaten egg.

Brown scones

I recently discovered that apple tart and Cheddar cheese is a thing, particularly in some parts of England. My Irish version of that – and my personal guilty pleasure – is a warm brown scone, some salted butter, orange marmalade and a strong mature Cheddar. I just adore it. Brown bread and marmalade is nothing new, but I love the extra crunch you get from dipping the top of the scones into mixed seeds before baking.

Makes 8

200g coarse wholemeal flour

200g self-raising flour

1 tsp baking powder

85g cold butter, cut into small pieces

220ml buttermilk

1 medium egg, beaten

mixed seeds, for the top

Preheat the oven to 200°C fan. Line a baking sheet with non-stick baking paper.

Place the flours and baking powder in a large bowl and mix well using your fingers. Add the butter and rub together until the mixture looks like fine breadcrumbs.

Add the buttermilk and mix together using a table knife to form a soft dough, adding a little more milk if needed.

Turn out onto a lightly floured surface. Lightly flour the top of the dough and gently bring it together. Using a rolling pin, roll out the dough to a thickness of 3cm. Use a 6cm round cutter to stamp out the scones. Lightly knead the trimmings together and roll and cut like before.

Place the scones on the lined baking sheet and brush the tops with the beaten egg. Either sprinkle with the mixed seeds or, as I prefer, dip the top into the mixed seeds. Bake in the preheated oven for about 15 minutes, until they are nicely risen and golden brown. Then if you're like me, slather the warm scone in salted butter and sweet orange marmalade and have it with a good strong Cheddar for the perfect bite.

Tear & share smoked garlic & cheese scones

Fluffy scones ✔ Melted cheese ✔ Garlic butter ✔ Warm smokiness ✔ This tear-and-share bake ticks all the right boxes, and believe me, once you've made it you'll be addicted. Serve this bake straight out of the oven while it's hot, molten and buttery.

Makes 12

350g self-raising flour

1 tsp baking powder

1 tsp smoked paprika

85g cold butter, cut into small pieces

140g Cheddar cheese – 65g grated, 75g cut into 12 cubes

1 small bunch of fresh parsley, finely chopped

salt and freshly ground black pepper

180ml buttermilk

For the garlic butter:

75g butter, very soft

4 cloves of smoked garlic, finely chopped

1 small bunch of fresh parsley, finely chopped

Preheat the oven to 180°C fan.

To make the garlic butter, simply blend the soft butter with the smoked garlic and chopped parsley. Liberally brush the bottom of a 23cm square ceramic baking dish or a baking tray lined with non-stick baking paper with half the garlic butter and set aside.

Place the flour, baking powder and smoked paprika in a large bowl and mix well using your fingers. Add the butter and rub together until the mixture looks like fine breadcrumbs.

Add the grated cheese and the parsley and season with salt and pepper. Use a table knife to stir them through, then add the buttermilk and mix together using the table knife to form a soft dough.

Turn out onto a lightly floured surface. Lightly flour the top of the dough and gently bring it together, then divide the dough into 12 pieces.

Using your thumb, push a dimple into the centre of a piece of dough and add a cube of cheese. Close the dough around the cheese and lightly roll into a ball. Repeat with the remaining dough pieces and cheese cubes.

Arrange the 12 balls of dough in the dish and brush with the remaining garlic butter. Bake in the preheated oven for 25 minutes. Serve warm.

I often make a double batch of the garlic butter (you can never have too much garlic butter!) and serve a little more on the side for extra indulgence.

Cakes & Bakes

Victoria sandwich

I have a French friend living here in Dublin, Katia Valadeau, who loves the smell of cakes, but she doesn't mean the sweet sugary smell – she talks of the smell of the free-range eggs and the butter. There is no cake better at releasing these aromas than this classic.

Serves 10

225g butter, softened, plus extra for greasing

225g caster sugar

225g self-raising flour

2 tsp baking powder

5 medium eggs

2 tbsp milk

1 tsp vanilla

To finish:

your favourite jam

softly whipped cream

icing sugar

1 batch of vanilla buttercream frosting (page 12, optional)

fresh edible flowers (optional: ask your florist if you aren't sure)

Preheat the oven to 180°C fan. Prepare 2 x 20cm cake tins by lightly greasing the sides and lining the bottoms with non-stick baking paper.

Put all the cake ingredients in a large bowl. Using an electric hand mixer or a stand mixer fitted with the paddle attachment, mix well until all the ingredients are combined and the batter is light and fluffy.

Divide the batter between the two tins and bake in the preheated oven for 20–25 minutes. The cakes should be a nice golden colour, coming away slightly from the sides of the tin, and have a slight spring to the touch. Allow to cool in the tins for about 5 minutes before turning out onto a wire rack to cool completely.

To assemble, place the first sponge upside down on a plate and top with a generous layer of your favourite jam, then an even more generous layer of whipped cream (though personally, I prefer to serve the whipped cream on the side rather than in between the sponges). Place the second sponge on top and dust with icing sugar. If you want to go old school, place a paper doily on top of the cake before you dust it with the icing sugar for a retro finish.

If you would like to make this cake extra special, include a layer of vanilla buttercream frosting in the centre of the cake with the jam and decorate the top with fresh flowers.

PB&J sandwich

As a contrast to the Victoria sandwich, I wanted to take inspiration from a real-life sandwich and make it into a cake. Peanut butter and jelly sandwiches are an American childhood classic dating back to the early 1900s. But in the US, jelly is not as we know it here – across the pond, jelly is a common name for jam or a fruit preserve. In my version, though, I use the Irish type of jelly, which in the States they call by its brand name, Jell-O – confused yet?

Serves 10

For the jelly layer:

500ml water

2 x 135g packs of jelly
(I use raspberry)

125g fresh raspberries,
cut in half (if you prefer
a different jelly, change
this to the appropriate
fresh fruit)

For the sponge:

225g caster sugar

225g self-raising flour

175g butter, softened

50g crunchy peanut
butter

2 tsp baking powder

5 medium eggs

2 tbsp milk

1 tsp vanilla

Start by making the jelly layer. Measure out 500ml water. Melt both packs of jelly as per the packet instructions, using water from the 500ml, then top up using the rest of the water.

Line a 23cm square baking tin with cling film, allowing it to drape over the sides. Arrange the fruit in the bottom of the lined tin and gently pour over the liquid jelly. Put in the fridge and allow to set completely. When it's firmly set, use the cling film to lift the jelly out of the tin and onto a chopping board. Return to the fridge until ready to use.

Meanwhile, to make the sponge, preheat the oven to 180°C fan. Prepare a 23cm square baking tin by lightly greasing the sides and lining the bottom with non-stick baking paper.

Put all the sponge ingredients in a large bowl. Using an electric hand mixer or a stand mixer fitted with the paddle attachment, mix well until all the ingredients are combined and the batter is light and fluffy.

Scrape the batter into the tin and smooth the top to flatten it slightly. Bake in the preheated oven for 25–30 minutes. The cake should be a nice golden colour, coming away slightly from the sides of the tin, and have a slight spring to the touch. Allow to cool in the tin for about 5 minutes before turning out onto a wire rack to cool completely.

To make the peanut butter frosting, use an electric hand mixer or a stand mixer fitted with the paddle attachment to whip the softened butter with the icing sugar, milk and vanilla. Start on a low speed before increasing it to high and continue to whip for about 5 minutes. ➔

For the peanut butter frosting:

125g butter, softened

250g icing sugar

4 tbsp milk

1 tsp vanilla

50g crunchy peanut butter

To finish:

100g raspberry jam

75g salted peanuts, roughly chopped

icing sugar, for dusting

Add the peanut butter for the last 30 seconds or so.

To assemble, cut the cake horizontally into two layers. Place the first sponge upside down on a plate and top with the peanut butter frosting. Add the jam, slightly swirling it into the frosting using your knife, then sprinkle with the roughly chopped peanuts. Using the cling film, gently place the jelly layer on top of the jam by lining up the edge of the jelly with the edge of the cake closest to you, then lay the jelly away from you. Remove the cling film and place the second sponge on top, then dust with icing sugar.

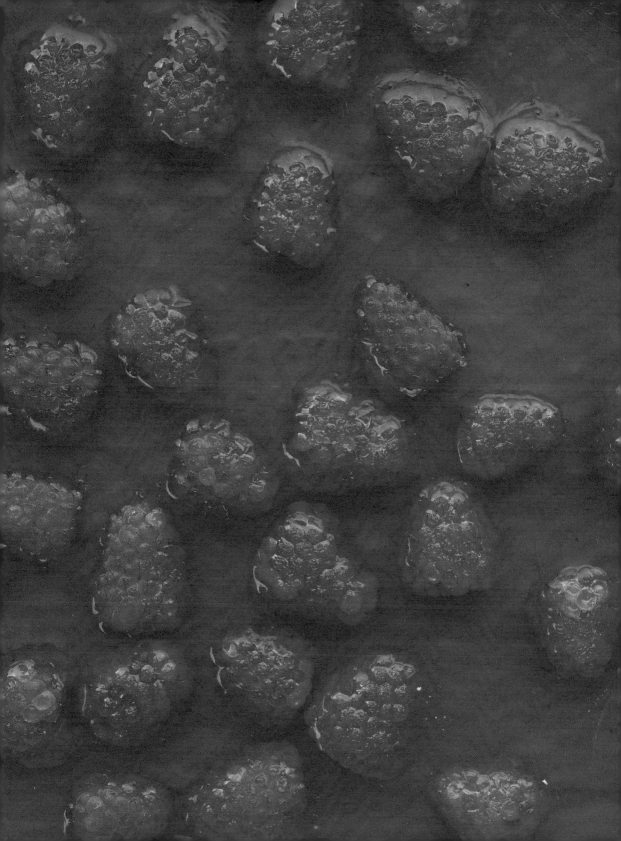

Coffee & walnut cake

I once asked people on Instagram to tell me what their favourite traditional bakes are and no bake was as popular – or caused as much controversy! – as coffee (and walnut) cake. People have so many memories of it: it was homemade; it was made by a relative; it was served in Arnott's Café; the best one was from the Tea Time Express. But there were also very different rules about ingredients, fillings and decoration: no walnuts, just coffee; made with real coffee; made with Nescafé Gold Blend; made with Irel coffee essence; iced with just buttercream; iced with buttercream and a glaze ... the possibilities are endless and everyone has their own favourite. This is mine.

Serves 10

225g butter, softened, plus extra for greasing

225g caster sugar

225g self-raising flour

2 tsp baking powder

5 medium eggs

2 tbsp coffee extract, Irel or Camp

1 tsp vanilla

50g walnuts, roughly chopped (optional)

For the coffee frosting:

150g butter, softened

300g icing sugar

3 tbsp coffee extract, Irel or Camp

To decorate:

10 whole walnuts

Preheat the oven to 180°C fan. Prepare 2 x 20cm cake tins by lightly greasing the sides and lining the bottoms with non-stick baking paper.

Place the butter, sugar, flour, baking powder, eggs, coffee and vanilla in a large bowl. Using an electric hand mixer or a stand mixer fitted with the paddle attachment, mix well until all the ingredients are combined and the batter is light and fluffy. Gently fold in the chopped walnuts (if using).

Divide the batter evenly between the two tins and bake in the preheated oven for 20–25 minutes. The cakes should be a nice golden colour, coming away slightly from the sides of the tins, and have a slight spring to the touch. Allow to cool in the tins for about 5 minutes before turning out onto a wire rack to cool completely.

To make the frosting, put the butter, icing sugar and coffee in a large bowl. Using a hand mixer or a stand mixer again, combine the ingredients slowly at first until everything is combined, then mix at a high speed for about 5 minutes, until everything is whipped to a light, fluffy, spreadable consistency.

Sandwich the cakes together with approximately one-third of the frosting, using the remainder to cover the sides and top. Decorate the top with the whole walnuts before serving.

Coffee & walnut pavlova
with coffee poached pears

When we were growing up, my mum used to do some private catering from home. One of her most popular desserts was (and still is) her pavlova. In memory of getting up early on Saturday mornings, 'shaving' kiwis and chopping fruit for the fillings, this one's for you, Mum. Love you!

Serves 8

4 medium egg whites

220g caster sugar

½ tsp cornflour

½ tsp white wine vinegar

100g chopped walnuts, plus extra to decorate

For the coffee poached pears:

8 ripe but firm pears

750g caster sugar

750ml freshly brewed black coffee

1 tsp vanilla

1 star anise

Preheat the oven to 110°C fan. Line two baking trays with non-stick baking paper. Draw a 20cm circle on each piece of paper with a pencil, then flip the paper over so that the outline is still visible – this way, the pencil markings won't be transferred to the bottom of your pavlova.

In a spotlessly clean, dry bowl, whisk the egg whites until soft peaks form. While still whisking, gradually add the sugar and whisk until it becomes thick and glossy, then whisk in the cornflour and vinegar. Gently fold in the walnuts.

Divide the meringue between the two prepared baking trays, spreading it out neatly into the circle outline that you drew on the paper. Bake in the preheated oven for 1 hour, then turn off the heat and let the pavlova cool completely inside the oven with the door slightly ajar.

Meanwhile, to prepare the poached pears, you'll need a saucepan that's big enough to hold the pears tightly standing upright. Peel the pears and cut a bit off the bottom of each pear so that they stand up nicely in the pan and on the pavlova.

Add the sugar, coffee, vanilla and star anise and bring to the boil, then reduce the heat and simmer gently for 10 minutes to allow the flavours to infuse before carefully adding the pears, standing them upright. Cover the pan and gently poach for about 30 minutes, until the pears are soft. ➔

For the coffee mascarpone cream:

500ml cream

2 tsp icing sugar

250g mascarpone cheese

2 tbsp coffee extract, Irel or Camp

Remove the pan from the heat and allow to cool. The pears can be poached up to two days ahead and kept in the fridge in the cooking liquor.

To make the coffee mascarpone cream, whip the cream and icing sugar in a large bowl until soft peaks form. Put the mascarpone in a separate medium-sized bowl with the coffee essence and 2 tablespoons of the whipped cream and mix to loosen it slightly (this will make it easier to fold into the remaining softly whipped cream). Gently fold the mascarpone mixture into the whipped cream until thoroughly combined.

To assemble, place one of the pavlovas on a serving plate and spread with half of the coffee mascarpone cream. Place the second meringue on top and cover with the remaining cream and the coffee poached pears (left whole or cut into wedges). Scatter over some chopped walnuts to decorate.

Chocolate cake

I still remember the chocolate cake I got from Crotty's Bakery in Carlow town for my seventh birthday. The reason it sticks out in my memory is because of the thick disc of chocolate on top that had my name written on it. The whole cake was a complete chocolate overload and I loved it! Inspired by that cake, I've finished this cake with shards of chocolate for that extra chocolatey kick.

Serves 8

butter, for greasing

250g self-raising flour

45g cocoa powder

1 tsp bread soda

200g caster sugar

200ml oil (vegetable, sunflower or rapeseed)

200ml milk

3 medium eggs, beaten

3 tbsp golden syrup

For the icing:

250g butter, softened

500g icing sugar

50g cocoa powder

4 tbsp milk

Preheat the oven to 170°C fan. Grease and line the bases of two 20cm round sandwich tins with a little butter.

Sift the flour, cocoa powder and bread soda into a large bowl, then mix in the caster sugar. Make a well in the centre of the dry ingredients and add all the wet ingredients. Mix really well using a hand mixer or a stand mixer fitted with the paddle attachment until you have a smooth batter.

Divide the batter evenly between the two tins (approximately 500g in each tin). Bake in the preheated oven for 35 minutes, until firm to the touch. Allow to cool in the tins for 15 minutes before turning out onto wire racks to cool completely.

To make the icing, put the butter, icing sugar, cocoa and milk in a large bowl. Using a hand mixer or a stand mixer again, beat the ingredients slowly at first until everything is combined, then mix at a high speed for about 5 minutes, until everything is whipped to a light, fluffy, spreadable consistency.

Sandwich the cakes together with approximately one-third of the icing, using the remainder to cover the sides and top.

To make the chocolate decorations, place the chocolate in a heatproof bowl set over a pan of gently simmering water, making sure the water doesn't touch the bottom of the bowl (see page 14 for more info on melting chocolate).

Place a piece of non-stick baking paper on a cutting board and use a pencil to draw a circle slightly smaller than the cake on it, then flip the paper over so that the outline is still visible – this way, the pencil markings won't be transferred to the bottom of your chocolate. ➔

To decorate:

120g milk chocolate, roughly chopped

sprinkles, dragées and/ or sugar decorations

Pour the melted chocolate into the middle of the circle, then use a teaspoon or palette knife to encourage the chocolate to the edge of the circle. Decorate the melted chocolate circle with some sprinkles, dragées or any other sugar decorations you like. Just before the chocolate has completely hardened, cut the circle into eight wedges. Once the chocolate is completely hard, use these wedges to decorate the cake.

Chocolate stout cake
with honeycomb whiskey frosting

The first time I tasted the Salted Caramel Pastry Stout from the White Hag Brewing Company in Sligo, I just knew I had to make a cake with it. In a serendipitous moment, the following day, Lisa from the Dublin Liberties Distillery introduced me to their Irish Whiskey and Honeycomb Liqueur. That was it – these two just had to be married in cake!

Serves 8

200g butter

100g cocoa powder

150ml White Hag Brewing Co. Salted Caramel Pastry Stout (or a regular stout)

250g plain flour

2 tsp baking powder

350g caster sugar

200ml sour cream

2 medium eggs, beaten

1 tsp vanilla

For the honeycomb whiskey frosting:

150g butter, softened

300g icing sugar

4 tbsp Dubliner Irish Whiskey and Honeycomb Liqueur (or Irish Mist or regular whiskey)

To decorate:

2 honeycomb chocolate bars, broken into pieces

Preheat the oven to 160°C fan. Grease and line the base of a 20cm round springform tin.

Melt the butter in a saucepan over a low heat. Remove the pan from the heat, then add the cocoa powder and stout, mixing well.

Sift the flour and baking powder into a large bowl, then stir in the sugar. Make a well in the centre of the dry ingredients and add the stout mixture, sour cream, eggs and vanilla. Mix well using a hand mixer or a stand mixer fitted with the paddle attachment until you have a smooth batter.

Pour the batter into the prepared tin. Bake in the preheated oven for 50–60 minutes, until firm to the touch. Allow to cool in the tin for 15 minutes before releasing the sides of the tin, then transfer to a wire rack to cool completely.

To make the frosting, put the butter, icing sugar and liqueur in a large bowl. Using a hand mixer or a stand mixer again, combine the ingredients slowly at first until everything is combined, then mix at a high speed for about 5 minutes, until everything is whipped to a light, fluffy, spreadable consistency.

Pile the frosting on top of the cooled cake and spread to the edges using a palette knife or spoon. Decorate with the broken honeycomb chocolate bars.

No-bake berry cheesecake

I feel like a bit of a fraud adding a no-bake cake into a book about baking, but I simply love a berry cheesecake. If you are from my hometown of Athy and of a certain age, you might remember me or my brothers selling strawberries on the side of the street outside Shaws department store. The mad thing about it is that at the time, I didn't know that I'm allergic to strawberries. So now when I make this cheesecake for myself it doesn't contain any strawberries, but that doesn't need to stop you from adding them.

Serves 8–10

160g digestive biscuits, finely crushed

45g butter, melted

400g cream cheese

75g icing sugar

1 tbsp vanilla

1 tbsp lemon juice

300ml cream

150g mixed fresh berries (strawberries, blackberries, raspberries, blueberries, etc.), finely chopped

To serve:

150g mixed fresh berries

1 tbsp icing sugar

½ tbsp lemon juice

fresh mint sprigs

Line the bottom of a 20cm springform tin with non-stick baking paper.

Put the crushed biscuits and melted butter in a bowl and stir until evenly combined, then scrape into the bottom of the prepared tin. Use the back of a spoon to evenly press the crumbs into the base of the tin. Allow to chill and firm up in the fridge for about 1 hour.

To make the filling, put the cream cheese, icing sugar, vanilla and lemon juice in a bowl and use a hand mixer or a stand mixer fitted with the paddle attachment to combine. Pour in the cream and beat for a further minute or so, until the mixture has thickened. Gently fold in the chopped berries.

Pour the cheesecake mixture on top of the prepared base, using a spoon or palette knife to level it out. Chill in the fridge for at least 2 hours.

In the meantime, mix the berries with the icing sugar and lemon juice and set aside to macerate.

To serve, release the cheesecake from the springform tin. You can either pile the macerated berries on top and decorate with a few fresh mint sprigs before cutting into slices or you can serve the berries on the side.

Yes-bake lemon meringue cheesecake

What do you get if you cross a baked cheesecake with a lemon meringue pie? You get this! Sometimes you really don't have to reinvent the wheel, but there is nothing wrong with taking two beautiful wheels and making something even more beautiful. I first created this recipe for *The Six O'Clock Show* a few years ago, but like many of my recipes, I have revisited it and made little tweaks since then to really up the zesty lemon flavour.

Serves 8–10

200g lemon puff biscuits, broken into crumbs

75g butter, melted

640g cream cheese

200ml sour cream

200g caster sugar

3 medium egg yolks

1 medium egg

3 lemons – zest from all 3 and juice from 1

1½ tsp vanilla

100g lemon curd

For the meringue:

3 medium egg whites

90g caster sugar

Preheat the oven to 160°C fan. Line the bottom and sides of a 20cm springform tin with non-stick baking paper.

Put the crushed biscuits and melted butter in a bowl and stir until evenly combined, then scrape into the bottom of the prepared tin. Use the back of a spoon to evenly press the crumbs into the base of the tin.

Whisk the cream cheese and sour cream together until smooth. Add the sugar, egg yolks and the whole egg, then add the lemon zest and juice and the vanilla and continue to whisk until everything is combined. Pour the cheesecake filling onto the biscuit base.

Bake in the preheated oven for 55–60 minutes. To check that it's done, the cheesecake should feel set but still have a slight wobble in the centre. Take it out of the oven and place on a wire rack to cool completely before releasing the cheesecake from the tin. Top with the lemon curd and put it in the fridge.

To make the meringue, whisk the egg whites in a spotlessly clean, dry bowl with an electric hand mixer or a stand mixer fitted with the whisk attachment until you have soft peaks. Gradually add the sugar one-third at a time, whisking until the meringue is thick and glossy.

There are two ways to finish the meringue: either in a hot oven or using a kitchen blowtorch.

To finish in the oven, spread the meringue on top of the chilled cheesecake and bake in the oven preheated to 180°C for 10–15 minutes, until golden.

To finish with a kitchen blowtorch, take the cheesecake
out of the fridge 20–30 minutes before eating. Spread
the meringue on top of the cheesecake and use the
blowtorch to lightly toast the meringue.

Swiss roll

As I was writing this recipe, I suddenly remembered watching my sister make Swiss rolls when we were kids. I rang her to ask her about it and she said that it was something she used to do with our Granny Flynn – the same granny who taught me to make tea brack. You'd be hard pressed to find many other baking recipes that are as classic and simple as this one, but isn't it incredible how just four ingredients can keep memories and family connections alive over the years?

Serves 8

4 medium eggs

100g caster sugar, plus extra for sprinkling

100g self-raising flour

200g jam

Preheat the oven to 160°C fan. Line a 25cm x 38cm Swiss roll tin with non-stick baking paper.

Put the eggs and sugar in a large bowl. Using an electric hand mixer or a stand mixer fitted with the whisk attachment, whisk for about 10 minutes, until the mixture is thick and pale and leaves a ribbon when you remove the beaters or whisk.

Sift half of the flour into the egg mixture and gently fold it in using a large metal spoon, then repeat with the remaining flour. Take your time and be gentle doing this to keep as much air as possible in the sponge mixture.

Pour the batter into the prepared tin and use a palette knife to spread it into the corners. Bake in the middle shelf of the preheated oven for 12–15 minutes, until golden and just firm to the touch.

While it's baking, lay a clean damp tea towel on your work surface. Put a piece of non-stick baking paper that's bigger than the Swiss roll tin on top of the towel, then sprinkle some extra caster sugar all over the paper. Give the jam a good stir to make it more spreadable – you can heat it ever so slightly in a saucepan or in the microwave if required.

When the sponge is cooked, turn it out onto the sugar-coated paper so that the top of the sponge is now pressed against the sugar. Peel off the baking paper from the bottom of the sponge, which is now facing up. Spread the jam all over the sponge but leave a thin border (about 2cm) clear on each side.

Lifting the paper edge that's closest to you, gently start rolling up the sponge, using the paper to help you roll. It's easiest to do this while the sponge is still warm. Allow to cool completely, seam side down.

Trim off the ends to neaten up the roll before cutting into slices to serve.

Variations

ROLL
WITH IT

All you need is four simple ingredients to make a classic Swiss roll, but with a few little tweaks, the variations are endless.

LEMON
Add the zest of one lemon when folding in the flour and fill the Swiss roll with lemon curd instead of jam.

LIME & COCONUT
Add the zest of one lime when folding in the flour. Sprinkle the top of the sponge with desiccated coconut before baking and fill with lime marmalade instead of jam.

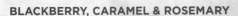

BLACKBERRY, CARAMEL & ROSEMARY

This was the flavour of my and Daithi's wedding cake, but to enjoy this amazing flavour combination at home, I've turned it into a Swiss roll. Add a very small amount of finely chopped fresh rosemary – say, ¼ teaspoon – when folding in the flour. Fill with blackberry jam and a drizzle of shop-bought caramel.

RHUBARB & GINGER

Add 1 teaspoon ground ginger when sifting the flour and fold in like normal. Fill with rhubarb jam.

CHOCOLATE & HAZELNUT

Replace 15g of the flour with 15g cocoa powder and fold it in as per the recipe. Fill with chocolate hazelnut spread, warmed slightly to make it more spreadable, and scatter some chopped roasted hazelnuts on top before rolling.

Matcha, mascarpone & white chocolate roulade

Matcha tea has the most unique flavour. It's botanical and slightly bitter, yet it also has a light, sweet finish with umami notes. This unique flavour paired with the creaminess of the mascarpone and the floral tones from the white chocolate works really well.

Serves 8

2 tbsp matcha powder

2 tbsp boiling water

4 medium eggs

100g caster sugar, plus extra to decorate

100g self-raising flour

For the filling:

75g white chocolate, roughly chopped

200ml cream

200g mascarpone cheese

25g caster sugar

To decorate:

matcha powder

fresh and dried raspberries

Preheat the oven to 160°C fan. Line a 25cm x 38cm Swiss roll tin with non-stick baking paper.

Make a paste by mixing the matcha powder with the boiling water.

Put the eggs and sugar in a large bowl. Using an electric hand mixer or a stand mixer fitted with the whisk attachment, whisk for about 10 minutes, until the mixture is thick and pale and leaves a ribbon when you remove the beaters or whisk. Add the matcha paste and mix for another minute.

Sift half of the flour into the egg mixture and gently fold it in using a large metal spoon, then repeat with the remaining flour. Take your time and be gentle doing this to keep as much air as possible in the sponge mixture.

Pour the batter into the prepared tin and use a palette knife to spread it into the corners. Bake in the middle shelf of the preheated oven for 12–15 minutes, until golden and just firm to the touch.

While it's baking, lay a clean damp tea towel on your work surface. Put a piece of non-stick baking paper that's bigger than the Swiss roll tin on top of the towel, then sprinkle some extra caster sugar all over the paper.

When the sponge is cooked, turn it out onto the sugar-coated paper so that the top of the sponge is now pressed against the sugar. Peel off the baking paper from the bottom of the sponge, which is now facing up. Cover with another sheet of non-stick baking paper and allow to cool completely. ⊕

To make the filling, melt the white chocolate in a heatproof bowl set over a pan of gently simmering water, making sure the water doesn't touch the bottom of the bowl. Once it has melted, remove the bowl from the pan and set aside to let the chocolate cool a little. (See page 14 for more info on melting chocolate.)

Lightly whip the cream in a medium-sized bowl. In a separate bowl, lighten the mascarpone by mixing it with the sugar and 2 tablespoons of the whipped cream, then gently fold in the rest of the whipped cream. Finally, fold in the melted white chocolate. Reserve some of this mixture to decorate the top of the roulade.

Spread the mascarpone filling all over the cooled sponge but leave a thin border of sponge (about 2cm) clear on either side.

Lifting the paper edge that's closest to you, gently start rolling up the sponge, using the paper to help you roll. Trim off the ends to neaten the roll, then decorate with a dusting of matcha powder, the reserved cream mixture and the raspberries. Cut into slices to serve.

Banana bread
with maple & cinnamon glaze

This bake has become so popular over the past few years, even going viral during the pandemic lockdowns in 2020, when we were all looking for some good old-fashioned comfort. It's quite a simple bake, so I've elevated it a little with a maple and cinnamon glaze. I think it's a fantastic bake to get children involved with, so get baking and make some special memories.

Makes 1 x 900g (2lb) loaf

110g butter, softened

225g caster sugar

2 medium eggs, beaten

3 very ripe bananas, mashed

90ml buttermilk

1 tsp vanilla

190g plain flour

100g coarse wholemeal flour

1 tsp bread soda

40g pecan nuts

½ tsp ground cinnamon

For the maple and cinnamon glaze:

100g icing sugar, sifted

25g butter, very soft

3 tbsp maple syrup

½ tsp ground cinnamon

½ tsp vanilla

To decorate:

a handful of pecans

a handful of dried banana chips

Preheat the oven to 180°C fan. Line a 900g (2lb) loaf tin with non-stick baking paper.

Cream the butter and sugar together until the mixture is light and fluffy, then mix in the beaten eggs.

Add the mashed bananas, buttermilk and vanilla. Mix well. Fold in both the flours, the bread soda, pecans and cinnamon until everything is well combined.

Pour into the prepared tin and bake in the preheated oven for 50–60 minutes. To check that the loaf is cooked, a skewer inserted into the middle should come out clean. Allow to cool in the tin for about 15 minutes before removing from the tin to cool completely on a wire rack.

The loaf is perfectly fine to eat at this stage, but I love to top it with a glaze. Simply mix all the glaze ingredients together until you have a thick, smooth glaze, adding a little more icing sugar if it's too runny or a little more syrup if it's too thick. Spread the glaze over the loaf and scatter over the pecans and dried banana chips to decorate.

Apricot, carrot & orange loaf
with goats' cheese frosting

I simply adore goats' cheese and one of my favourites is St Tola, made by Siobhán Ni Ghairbith and her team in Ennistymon, County Clare. Her Divine goats' cream cheese is perfect for this recipe – it's divine by name and by nature!

Makes 1 x 900g (2lb) loaf

120g dried apricots, thinly sliced

zest and juice of 1 orange

200g dark brown sugar

175g self-raising flour

2 tsp sweet spice (page 15) or mixed spice

½ tsp bread soda

½ tsp salt

140ml vegetable oil

2 medium eggs, beaten

300g peeled and grated carrots

80g walnuts, roughly chopped

For the goats' cheese frosting:

150g icing sugar, sifted

75g butter, softened

150g soft goats' cheese or cream cheese

To decorate:

fresh or dried edible flower petals

Start by soaking the sliced apricots in the orange zest and juice for about 1 hour.

Preheat the oven to 140°C fan. Line a 900g (2lb) loaf tin with non-stick baking paper

Mix the brown sugar, flour, spice, bread soda and salt together in a large bowl. Make a well in the centre and add the apricot and orange mixture along with the oil, eggs, grated carrots and walnuts, mixing until well combined.

Pour into the prepared tin and bake in the preheated oven for 65–75 minutes. To check that the loaf is cooked, a skewer inserted into the middle should come out clean. Allow to cool in the tin for about 15 minutes before removing from the tin to cool completely on a wire rack.

To make the frosting, use an electric hand mixer or a stand mixer fitted with the paddle attachment to combine the icing sugar and butter. Continue to mix until you have a light, fluffy frosting, then reduce the speed of your mixer and add the goats' cheese or cream cheese and mix until just combined – don't overmix or it could turn runny.

Spread the frosting over the cooled loaf and decorate with fresh or dried edible flowers.

Irish porter cake

This is not something we had very often growing up because it was more about tea brack in my family. My husband, on the other hand, has great memories of porter cake and after a little persuasion his mammy, Monica, has shared the recipe with me and now you in turn. Her original recipe is in imperial measurements and is for a 23cm tin. I've taken inspiration from her recipe, converted it to metric and reduced it ever so slightly to fit a 20cm tin. The photo of this porter cake perfectly sums up spending time at my in-laws' house. There is always a pot of tea on the go and we sit around the kitchen table chatting with a cuppa and something homemade. Monica, thank you.

Serves 12–15

400g mixed dried fruit (raisins, currants, sultanas, mixed peel)

175g butter

200g light brown sugar

200ml porter or stout, preferably from a bottle

zest and juice of 1 lemon

400g plain flour, sifted

50g glacé cherries, cut in half

3 medium eggs, beaten

1 tsp sweet spice (page 15) or mixed spice

½ tsp ground nutmeg

½ tsp ground cinnamon

1 tsp bread soda

½ tsp salt

Put the mixed dried fruit, butter, brown sugar, porter or stout and the lemon zest and juice in a saucepan and bring to the boil, then reduce the heat and simmer for 10 minutes. Take the pan off the heat and allow to cool.

Preheat the oven to 150°C fan. Line a 20cm cake tin with non-stick baking paper.

Pour the fruit and porter mixture into a large mixing bowl, then add the flour, cherries, eggs, spices, bread soda and salt. Gently mix together using a wooden spoon. The batter should have a dropping consistency – if it feels a little stiff and dry, add an extra splash of porter.

Transfer the cake batter into the prepared tin and bake in the preheated oven for 1½–2 hours. To check that the cake is cooked, a skewer inserted into the middle should come out clean.

Allow to cool in the tin for about 15 minutes before turning out onto a wire rack. This cake is best left to mature for a few days in an airtight container before serving.

West Indies porter cake

I love taking inspiration from products I come across, so when I first tasted the Guinness West Indies Porter, I immediately thought of using it to make a version of a classic porter cake. I've used tropical fruit like coconut and papaya, spices like nutmeg and ginger and a little rum in this version, bringing some Caribbean flavours to the cake.

Serves 12–15

350g mixed dried fruit (raisins, currants, sultanas, mixed peel)

50g dried apricots, cut into small pieces

175g butter

200g dark brown sugar

200ml Guinness West Indies Porter

zest and juice of 1 orange

400g plain flour, sifted

50g dried papaya, diced

50g dried coconut flakes, plus extra for the top

3 medium eggs, beaten

2–3 tbsp spiced rum

1 tsp sweet spice (page 15) or mixed spice

1 tsp ground ginger

½ tsp freshly grated nutmeg

1 tsp bread soda

½ tsp salt

Put the mixed dried fruit, apricots, butter, brown sugar, porter and the orange zest and juice in a saucepan and bring to the boil, then reduce the heat and simmer for 10 minutes. Take the pan off the heat and allow to cool.

Preheat the oven to 150°C fan. Line a 20cm cake tin with non-stick baking paper.

Pour the fruit and porter mixture into a large mixing bowl, then add the flour, papaya, coconut, eggs, rum, spices, bread soda and salt. Gently mix together using a wooden spoon. The batter should have a dropping consistency – if it feels a little stiff and dry, add an extra splash of porter.

Transfer the cake batter into the prepared tin and sprinkle some extra coconut flakes on top. Bake in the preheated oven for 1½–2 hours. To check that the cake is cooked, a skewer inserted into the middle should come out clean

Allow to cool in the tin for about 15 minutes before turning out onto a wire rack. This cake is best left to mature for a few days in an airtight container before serving.

Brack & Butter

BAKING
Brack

WITH GRANNY FLYNN

One of my earliest food memories is my **Granny Flynn** soaking fruit for a tea brack. I remember sitting at a marbled blue **Formica** table in her kitchen as she explained what she was doing, weighing her dried fruit and mixed peel into an iconic **Mason Cash** bowl. The tea was always **Campbell's** loose leaf from its yellow tin and most importantly, Granny Flynn told me that the tea should be **almost cold**. I was only 10 years old when my Granny Flynn passed away, but I owe so much to her for introducing me to the world of **baking** – and more specifically, the world of **brack**. That's why this Brack & Butter chapter is the **heart** of the book, both literally and figuratively.

Traditional tea brack

There are many ways to serve brack, but the most traditional one of all is a good thick slice with an equally impressive layer of good Irish butter. Another way I like to serve it is inspired by stories of my Grandad Flynn. At Christmastime, my mum would frequently remind us how he liked to fry a slice of Christmas pudding in some foaming butter on St Stephen's Day. I love that idea and have tried it, and it is delicious. But Christmas pudding isn't something I'd have lying around during the year, so brack fried in butter is a fantastic alternative, especially when served with ice cream or a spoonful of crème fraîche.

Makes 1 x 900g (2lb) loaf

300g sultanas

75g mixed peel

300g almost cold tea (see the note)

125g caster sugar

1 medium egg, lightly beaten

zest of 1 lemon

1 tsp sweet spice (page 15) or mixed spice

1 tsp vanilla

225g self-raising flour

Put the sultanas, mixed peel and tea in a large bowl and leave to soak overnight at room temperature.

When you're ready to bake, preheat the oven to 180°C fan. Line a 900g (2lb) loaf tin with non-stick baking paper.

Add the sugar, egg, lemon zest, spice and vanilla to the fruit and tea and mix well. Gently mix in the flour, being careful not to crush the fruit. Transfer to the lined loaf tin.

Bake in the preheated oven for 60–65 minutes. It's done when a skewer inserted into the centre of the loaf comes out clean. Allow to cool fully in the tin before cutting into slices – see pages 112–113 for some topping ideas, but you can't beat a cup of tea and a slice of brack spread with good butter.

Note

I don't bother measuring the tea in millilitres in a measuring jug since I already have the scale out anyway. Plus it saves on the washing up!

Malted coffee, chocolate & pecan brack

'Tea or coffee?' It's one of the first things you're asked when you call to someone's house in Ireland or meet a friend in a café, so I've given a traditional tea brack a coffee makeover. I've also added malt, chocolate and pecans to further bring this classic bang up to date. You can normally find barley malt extract in health food shops but if you can't get it, you could use a malt drink powder instead, which you'll find in most supermarkets. Instead of the barley malt extract, substitute 1 tablespoon malt drink powder dissolved in 2 teaspoons cold water.

Makes 1 x 900g (2lb) loaf

300g sultanas

50g pitted dates, roughly chopped

25g pecans, chopped, plus extra for the top

300g almost cold coffee (see the note)

125g light brown sugar

25g dark chocolate, chopped

1 medium egg, beaten

1 tbsp barley malt extract (or see the intro)

1 tsp vanilla

225g self-raising flour

To serve:

butter, ricotta or mascarpone cheese

Place the sultanas, dates, pecans and coffee in a large bowl and leave to soak overnight at room temperature.

When you're ready to bake, preheat the oven to 180°C fan. Line a 900g (2lb) loaf tin with non-stick baking paper.

Add the brown sugar, chocolate, egg, barley malt extract and vanilla to the fruit and coffee and mix well. Gently mix in the flour, being careful not to crush the fruit. Transfer to the lined loaf tin.

Bake in the preheated oven for 60–65 minutes. It's done when a skewer inserted into the centre of the loaf comes out clean. Allow to cool fully in the tin before cutting into slices.

Serve with butter or a soft creamy cheese like ricotta or mascarpone.

Note

I don't bother measuring the coffee in millilitres in a measuring jug since I already have the scale out anyway. Plus it saves on the washing up!

Barmbrack

As you have no doubt sussed by now, I am obsessed with tea brack and actually feel quite hurt when people refer to tea brack as barmbrack. Tea brack is very much a year-round thing, not just for Halloween. It's believed that the word *brack* comes from the Irish word *breac*, which means speckled, while the word *barm* refers to the foam formed on fermenting ale, which contains yeasts and cultures used in brewing. This barm became used as a raising agent when baking bread. For me, there are three key differences between barmbrack and tea brack. First, barmbrack is made with an enriched yeast dough shaped into a round, while tea brack is loaf shaped and relies on raising agents for its lift. Second, barmbrack doesn't contain any tea, while tea brack, well, I think the name speaks for itself. Last and by no means least, a barmbrack is traditionally eaten at Halloween and contains charms that are meant to tell your future, whereas tea brack is a year-round treat and never contains charms.

Serves 10–12

500g strong white flour

60g caster sugar

30g butter

1 x 7g sachet of fast-action dried yeast

2 tsp sweet spice (page 15) or mixed spice

½ tsp salt

150ml milk, warmed slightly

150ml water, warmed slightly

1 egg, beaten

400g mixed dried fruit

1 tbsp marmalade, warmed

Grease and line a deep 20cm cake tin.

Combine the flour, sugar, butter, yeast, spice and salt in the bowl of a stand mixer fitted with the dough hook. Slowly add the milk, water and the beaten egg, mixing until you have a soft dough. Continue to knead in the mixer for about for about 8 minutes, until the dough is smooth and feels stretchy. (You can mix and knead the dough by hand if you prefer.) Add the dried fruit and knead for a further minute.

Shape the dough into a round and place in the prepared cake tin. Cover with a clean damp tea towel and leave to rise for 1 hour.

Preheat the oven to 180°C fan.

Bake the barmbrack in the preheated oven for 45–50 minutes. When it's done, it should have a nice golden colour and sound hollow when tapped on the bottom.

Allow to cool in the tin for 5 minutes before turning out onto a wire rack. Brush with the warmed marmalade and allow the brack to cool completely.

Traditionally, the charms in a Halloween barmbrack would have been:

Pea: You will not marry within the year

Stick: Unhappy marriage or be in disputes

Piece of cloth: Bad luck and poor wealth

Coin: Good fortune

Ring: Wed within the year or good luck

Bean: A good future but with no money

Variations

DRESSED
BRACK

A simple slice of brack spread thickly with butter
is hard to beat, but it also works really well as an
accompaniment to a cheese board, particularly with
soft goats' cheese, blue cheese and strong mature
Cheddar. I have taken this idea one step further and
created dressed brack: individual slices of brack with
an elaborate combination of toppings to bring brack
to a whole new level.

Here are some examples to inspire you, but please
feel free to try your own combinations. A slice of
dressed brack is a wonderful addition to a dinner
party and makes a unique cheese course. It works
equally well on a picnic with all the different toppings
kept separate so that people can make up their
own slice. I know these might all seem a bit cheffy,
but don't be afraid to get creative with your own
combinations.

Corleggy Drumlin cheese,
Wooded Pig fennel salami,
compressed apple, confit fennel

St Tola goats' cheese, raspberries,
dried edible flower petals, rose and
raspberry gel, toasted almonds

Knockatee Kerry blue cheese,
fresh and dried figs, roast
walnuts, honey, bee pollen

Spiced brack butter, tea-poached pears,
lemon and vanilla mascarpone, whiskey-
soaked golden raisins, fresh thyme

Homemade butter

Ireland is lucky to have such a wonderful heritage of dairy production. We even have a butter museum in Shandon, County Cork. Some of my favourite Irish butter producers are Glenstal, Cuinneog, Abernethy, Glenilen, Ór, Irish Gourmet, Toonsbridge and Gloun Cross Dairy. I'm not going to pretend that I make a lot of butter or that I even have my own recipe – I will leave that in the very capable hands of Drs Sally and John McKenna. Their recipe for making butter in their book *Milk* is just perfect and they've shared it with me to include here in my own book. Please do check out their book if you would like to learn about and cook more food inspired by the amazing dairy we have in Ireland.

2 litres double cream, at room temperature

If you over-whip cream in a mixer, what you get is butter and buttermilk. For butter is simply whipped cream that collapses and separates into globules of butterfat and the milk that separates from it.

Place 2 litres of room temperature double cream in the bowl of a stand mixer and beat – using the whisk attachment – at medium speed. The cream will be softly, then stiffly whipped, and then it will go a step further and separate into buttermilk and butter.

The next step is to remove as much of the buttermilk as possible, as leaving it in will sour your butter. Turn the mixture out into a large square of muslin resting in a sieve over a bowl and press to remove the buttermilk into the bowl below.

Place the butter back in the mixer bowl. Whisk again for a few seconds to expel more buttermilk. Once again, strain and squeeze.

Fill a bowl with very cold water and put in the butter. Using your hands, knead the butter once more to remove more buttermilk. Replace the water and knead out more buttermilk. Eventually you will have a good butterfat mixture with no liquid. Salt the butter if you wish, adding 3 teaspoons to the mixture and rubbing in with your hands to distribute.

Note

For spreadable butter, simply leave it out at room temperature for an hour.

Flavoured brack butters

I love to have a slice of brack or toasted bread with some flavoured butter. Here are a few I like to make. Simply add the following to your favourite butter.

120g butter, softened

Spiced orange butter:

zest of 1 orange

2 tsp sweet spice (page 15) or mixed spice

Lemon and almond butter:

zest of 1 lemon

30g toasted flaked almonds, finely chopped

Hot toddy butter:

zest of ½ lemon

2 tbsp whiskey

6–8 whole cloves

½ tsp ground cloves

Beat the butter with a wooden spoon until it's soft and creamy, then beat in all the ingredients from one of the flavour combinations.

Scrape the butter out onto a square of baking paper or cling film, then shape the butter into a sausage by rolling it up in the paper or cling film. Twist the ends to seal and compact the butter. Chill the butter in the fridge for 1 hour before using. The butter will keep in the fridge for up to four days or can be frozen for up to one month.

Digestives & butter

There is a bit of a theme going on in this book: putting some kind of dairy on top of things. In this case, it's butter. Sometimes all a good butter needs is a simple carrier and here it's the crunchy, slightly sweet wholesomeness of homemade digestive biscuits. A digestive and butter with a cup of tea has a special place in my heart, as it reminds me of night-time chats with my mum when I was a teenager.

Makes 16 biscuits

250g coarse wholemeal flour, plus extra for dusting

1 tsp baking powder

½ tsp salt

90g light brown sugar

120g butter, chilled and diced

65ml milk

To serve:

softened butter

Preheat the oven to 180°C fan. Line two baking trays with non-stick baking paper.

Simply put all the ingredients except the milk in a food processor and whizz for about 1 minute, until well combined. Add the milk and pulse for another few seconds, just until the dough has come together.

Turn out onto a lightly floured surface and bring together to form a smooth ball. Using an extra dusting of flour, roll out the dough to a thickness of just over 5mm and stamp out into 8cm rounds. Gather the scraps together and repeat until all the dough is used up.

Divide the biscuits between the two lined baking trays. Prick the top of the biscuits all over with the prongs of a fork to create some holes.

Bake in the preheated oven for 18–20 minutes, until golden brown. Allow to cool on the baking trays for a few minutes before transferring to a wire rack with a palette knife to cool completely.

Spread with a little butter before eating.

Radishes & butter

I said in the previous recipe that good butter only needs a simple carrier, and it couldn't be simpler than this. I've used salted butter in almost every recipe in this book, but on this occasion please do seek out unsalted butter and please use the best radishes and salt that you can. I first ate radishes and butter on a holiday in the south of France with some friends while visiting Neasa Corish and her husband, Laurent Miquel, at their winery and family home. We shared an amazing meal with the Miquel family that also included prawns, lamb, crusty bread and, of course, lots of wine. Now whenever I have radishes and butter, it brings back those good memories of good times with Jacinta, Thierry, Eddie, Christine, David and Tracy.

Serves 4

1 bunch of radishes – try to use French breakfast radishes if you can

4 tbsp unsalted butter, cold but not hard

flaky sea salt

To serve:

warm bread (see the note)

a glass of Laurent Miquel Solas Viognier or rosé

Wash and trim the radishes, leaving some of the leaves attached. Arrange on a platter with the unsalted butter and flaky sea salt.

To eat, simply spread a little butter on the end of the radish (or halve the radishes and spread a little butter on the cut side) and sprinkle with a little sea salt for the perfect salty, creamy, crunchy bite. Enjoy with slices of good warm bread and a chilled glass of Laurent Miquel Solas Viognier or rosé.

Note

Use the simple white loaf recipe on page 40, but instead of shaping into a loaf after the second knead, divide the dough into 12 portions. Roll the individual pieces into balls and roll in some seeds of your choosing before leaving to prove for the second time for 25–30 minutes. Bake the individual rolls for 15–20 minutes.

Bread & butter pudding

This is still one of my favourite desserts when I'm back at home in my parents' house. A quick word of advice, though: if you have grown-up kids home for the weekend and they go out for a few drinks, hide the bread for the bread and butter pudding before they come home or else it will be toast. Literally. I still don't think my mum has forgiven us for eating all the bread that night!

Serves 6 (or 10 slices of toast)

60g caster sugar

4 medium eggs

300ml cream

250ml milk

1 tsp vanilla

zest of ½ lemon

10 slices of bread (stale day-old bread is perfect)

60g butter, softened, plus extra for greasing

60g dried fruit, such as raisins, sultanas or currants

Lightly grease a 23cm square or circular baking dish with butter.

Make the custard by mixing the sugar, eggs, cream, milk, vanilla and lemon zest in a large jug.

Spread all the slices of bread with the butter, then cut each slice in half diagonally to make triangles. Layer the slices of bread in the prepared dish and scatter the dried fruit across the top.

Give the custard mixture a final stir, then pour it over the bread. Allow to soak for 30 minutes.

Preheat the oven to 180°C fan.

Bake in the preheated oven for 35–40 minutes, until the custard is set and the top is golden brown. Serve warm.

(Or for the toast recipe, go to Paddy Dunne's pub with your husband, brother and his wife, then come back to the homestead and use an electric toaster to toast all the bread. Enjoy with lots of butter, mugs of tea and tipsy conversation.)

Brack & butter pudding

Over the past few years I have reinvented the humble tea brack in many guises. This is another rethink of both the tea brack and a traditional bread and butter pudding. I honestly don't think a brack will need using up in very many households. In our home, one certainly never lasts long enough for it to need to be used up before going stale. So I suggest you make two loaves of the traditional tea brack on page 106: one for this pudding and one to just enjoy with butter.

Serves 8–10 (this is a very rich dessert)

60g caster sugar

4 medium eggs

300ml cream

250ml milk

2 tbsp whiskey

1 tsp vanilla

zest of ½ orange

1 traditional tea brack (page 106), sliced

60g butter, softened, plus extra for greasing

To serve:

crème fraîche or softly whipped cream

Preheat the oven to 180°C fan. Lightly grease a 23cm square baking dish (or a roughly equivalent dish of another shape) with butter.

Make the custard by mixing the sugar, eggs, cream, milk, whiskey, vanilla and orange zest in a large jug.

Spread all the slices of brack with the butter, then cut each slice in half diagonally to make triangles. Layer the slices of bread in the prepared dish.

Give the custard mixture a final stir, then pour it over the brack. Allow to soak for 30 minutes.

Preheat the oven to 180°C fan.

Bake in the preheated oven for 35–40 minutes, until the custard is set and the top is golden brown. Serve warm with some crème fraîche or softly whipped cream.

Desserts & Treats

Apple sponge & custard

I love the emotion of food, from the comforting feeling you get from eating a favourite dish to the little thrill of trying something you've never had or heard of before. But if you ever want to feel like food is giving you a hug, then this is the dish for you. The hint of cinnamon and cardamom really brings home that warm, comforting, wholesome feeling.

Serves 6 generous hugs or 8 slightly more timid hugs!

450g cooking apples (roughly 2 large apples), peeled, cored and cut into bite-sized pieces

juice and zest of ½ lemon

1 tsp ground cinnamon

½ tsp ground cardamom

150g butter, softened, plus extra for greasing

150g caster sugar, plus 1 tbsp extra

150g self-raising flour

3 medium eggs, beaten

1 tsp vanilla

Preheat the oven to 180°C fan. Grease a 23cm square baking dish (or a roughly equivalent dish of another shape) with a little butter.

Put the apples in a large bowl with the lemon zest and juice and the spices. Mix well.

Put the butter, sugar, flour, eggs and vanilla in a separate bowl. Using an electric hand mixer or a stand mixer fitted with the paddle attachment, mix everything together until you have a smooth, well-combined, fluffy mixture – this will take a minute or two.

Stir the prepared apples into the batter and pour everything into the prepared dish. Bake in the preheated oven for 30–35 minutes, until the sponge mix has risen and has a nice golden colour.

Meanwhile, to make the custard, put the milk and cream in a heavy-based saucepan.

Cut the vanilla pod in half lengthways and gently scrape out the black seeds. Add the seeds and the pods to the milk. (This is the only time in the book that I recommend using a vanilla pod, but by all means, use 1 teaspoon of any vanilla you wish.) Place the pan on a medium heat and allow the milk mixture to come up to the boiling point, making sure to keep an eye on the pan so that the milk doesn't boil over (I've been there!). Remove the pan from the heat.

While the milk is heating, mix the egg yolks, sugar and cornflour together in a large bowl.

Once the milk has come up to the boil, carefully remove the vanilla pod from the milk. Slowly pour the hot milk into the sugar mixture, stirring constantly. Pour the custard back into the saucepan and put it back on a gentle heat. ➲

For the custard:

600ml milk

200ml cream

1 vanilla pod or 1 tsp of
any vanilla you wish

3 medium egg yolks

50g caster sugar

2 tbsp cornflour

Continue stirring until the custard has thickened enough to coat the back of a spoon. Don't allow the custard to boil.

Serve the warm custard with the hot apple sponge.

Toffee apple & doenjang caramel pudding

I absolutely love adding savoury ingredients into sweet dishes. In terms of taste, most people can differentiate between sweet, bitter, sour, salty and umami. The doenjang in this recipe – a fermented soybean paste from Korea – brings that slight umami flavour to the dish. When the brain recognises sweet and umami flavours together, it sees it as a pleasurable combination. When you think about it, almost all the recipes in this book have a umami element from the eggs used. This is a self-saucing pudding and will look completely wrong as you put it in the oven, but trust the process.

Serves 8

275g self-raising flour

140g caster sugar

1 tsp baking powder

3 medium eggs, beaten

100g butter, melted, plus extra for greasing

130ml milk

3 eating apples, peeled, cored and cut into bite-sized pieces

For the sauce:

200g light muscovado sugar

2 tbsp doenjang

350ml water, boiling

To serve:

cold softly whipped cream

Preheat the oven to 180°C fan. Grease a 23cm square baking dish (or a roughly equivalent dish of another shape) with butter.

Put the flour, caster sugar and baking powder in a large mixing bowl.

In a jug, mix together the eggs, melted butter and milk, then pour this into the dry ingredients and mix together until smooth. Stir in the apples, then scrape the batter into the greased baking dish and set aside.

To make the sauce, put the muscovado sugar and doenjang in a heatproof bowl or saucepan, then mix in the boiling water, stirring to allow the sugar to dissolve. Carefully pour this all over the pudding batter but don't be tempted to stir it in or do anything with it – just pour it on top of the batter and leave it alone. It will look VERY wrong at this stage, but don't panic!

Bake in the preheated oven for 30–35 minutes, until the surface looks firm, risen and crisp. Eat immediately with cold softly whipped cream.

Apple tart

When I think of apple tart, I think of Ruth Coyle. Ruth and her husband, Ernest, lived on the same street as us, Duke Street in Athy, when I was growing up. Ernest was a jeweller and watch maker and I remember watching him walk past our butcher shop at 3:00 p.m. every day as he went to wind the clock in the town hall. Ruth was like another mammy to me. She was so talented and creative in embroidery, painting, jam making and, most of all, baking. I can still remember the taste of her seasonal rhubarb, raspberry, and apple and blackberry tarts – some of my favourite flavours of my childhood.

Serves 8

plain flour, for dusting

2 batches of sweet shortcrust pastry (pages 14–15)

1 tbsp cornflour

750g cooking apples, peeled, cored and sliced

125g caster sugar, plus extra for sprinkling on top

6–8 cloves **or** ½ tsp ground cinnamon **or** zest of 1 lemon

1 medium egg, beaten

To serve:

softly whipped cream, ice cream or custard (pages 128–130)

Preheat the oven to 180°C fan. Lightly dust your countertop with a little flour.

Take just over half of the pastry and roll it out to line a 23cm pie dish. Sprinkle the cornflour over the bottom of the pastry in the pie dish – this will help to capture the juices from the apples during baking.

Put half of the apples into the pastry-lined dish, then sprinkle over half of the sugar and half of your flavouring of choice (cloves, cinnamon or lemon zest). Add the remaining apples and sprinkle with the remaining sugar and flavouring.

Brush the rim of the tart with a little beaten egg. Roll out the remaining pastry and lay it on top of the apples. Use the prongs of a fork to crimp and seal the two layers of pastry together. Trim any excess pastry from around the dish using a sharp knife. Brush the top with a little more beaten egg and sprinkle with some extra sugar.

Bake in the preheated oven for 45–55 minutes – the pastry should be a nice golden brown. Serve hot or cold with your choice of accompaniment, but mine is definitely whipped cream!

Gin, lemon & fuchsia tart

On an early June afternoon in 1994, when I was 16, my mum brought me over to Kildare town where we met Hilda O'Keefe, a great friend of my Aunt Yvonne. From Kildare I made the long journey with Hilda to Ballyferriter, County Kerry, where I spent the summer working in her sister Celeste's hotel, Óstan Dún an Óir. During that summer, my parents came down to stay. On one of the days we went to Dingle to eat in Benner's Hotel, where Hilda and Celeste's brother, Dano, was the manager. If I close my eyes and think about it, I can still taste the meal from that day: a main course of plaice stuffed with crabmeat and a dessert of rice pudding, dishes that my dad and I still talk about. I always think of that summer when I make the annual trip to Dingle for the Blas na hÉireann Irish Food Awards and the food festival. Inspired by the fuchsia-lined boreens of West Kerry and my love of gin, I've created this tart using Dingle Gin. It is also a thank you to Hilda, Celeste, Dano and all the O'Keefe family, who, unbeknownst to them, have played a huge part in my food journey – and, indeed, my life.

Serves 10

For the pastry:

6 juniper berries

200g plain flour, plus extra for dusting

100g butter, cold, plus extra for greasing

25g icing sugar

zest of ½ lemon

1 medium egg yolk

1 tbsp Dingle Gin or ice-cold water

To make the pastry, start by chopping the juniper berries as finely as you can. I find that if you squash them with the side of a knife first, it makes them easier to chop.

Put the chopped juniper berries, flour, butter, icing sugar and lemon zest in a food processor and pulse until it resembles fine breadcrumbs. Add the egg yolk and gin and pulse again just until the ingredients start to come together. Remove the dough from the food processor and use your hands to bring the pastry together into a ball. Flatten the pastry into a disc, wrap it in cling film and chill it in the fridge for about 30 minutes.

Grease a 23cm loose-bottomed tart tin and dust with flour. Lightly dust your countertop with flour too.

Place the pastry on the floured countertop and roll it out to a circle measuring roughly 28cm in diameter. Loosely roll the pastry around the rolling pin, then carefully unroll it into the tin. Gently press it into the corners and up the sides. Use a sharp knife to trim off any excess pastry. Place the unbaked tart in the fridge to chill for 30 minutes.

Preheat the oven to 160°C fan. ➔

For the filling:

225g caster sugar

5 medium eggs

125ml cream

4 tbsp Dingle Gin (see the note)

3 lemons – zest of 2½ and juice of all three

30g fuchsia flowers (see the note)

To blind bake the pastry, take a sheet of non-stick baking paper that is big enough to line the bottom and sides of the tin and scrunch it into a ball several times. This makes the paper a lot more pliable and it will fit better into the corners. Cover the pastry base with the paper and fill with uncooked rice or dried beans. Bake in the preheated oven for 15 minutes, then take the tart shell out of the oven and remove the rice or beans and the paper (keep the cooled rice or beans in a container for the next time you need to blind bake something). Return to the oven and bake for another 15 minutes. Allow to cool for 10 minutes on a wire rack.

Meanwhile, to make the filling, simply mix together the sugar, eggs, cream, gin, lemon zest and juice in a large bowl, then pour into a jug – this will make it easier to fill the tart.

Put the blind baked tart tin onto a baking sheet to make it easier to transfer to the oven. Give the filling mixture a good stir to distribute the zest, then pour half of it into the tart case. Arrange the fuchsia flowers in the mix, then carefully pour in the rest of the filling. You may find it easier to do this last step at the oven.

Bake in the preheated oven for 25–35 minutes, until just set – there should be a slight wobble in the centre when you lightly shake the tart. Allow to cool completely on a wire rack before cutting into slices to serve.

Note

You can of course use any gin you like as well as any edible flowers. Or if you want to leave out the gin altogether, use the zest of 3½ lemons and the juice of 4 lemons. If you are foraging for the fuchsia, be sure to pick it from locations that are well away from roadsides and wash the flowers in lightly salted water before using (the salted water will kill any bugs that might be hiding in the flowers!).

Rhubarb crumble

In early 2021, I came down with covid. It was a frightening time, not because I was sick (thankfully, my symptoms were mild), but because I lost the most valuable thing to a chef or baker: the ability to taste and smell. So I decided that I was going to use the opportunity of my isolation to discover more about what I enjoyed eating from a textural point of view. Both this recipe and the modern version on page 146 pick up on some of the things I learned about different sensations in one's mouth. While the chocolate, banana and coconut crumble with banana ice cream is all about the contrast between hot and cold, this recipe is more about texture – crispy, chewy and soft. By working the crumble topping a little bit further than you think it needs to go, you make nice little clusters that turn crispy or chewy during the cooking depending on whether they are towards the top of the crumble or touching the fruit, then under it all you get the soft fruit. I tend to make more crumble topping than I need and freeze the rest for another time. Freezing also helps the magical little clusters to stay together during baking – there is no need to defrost it, just use it straight from the freezer.

Serves 6

650g rhubarb, washed and cut into 5cm pieces

75–150g caster sugar (see the note on page 142)

1 tsp grated fresh ginger **or** ½ tsp ground ginger **or** 6 cubes of crystallised ginger, cut into small dice **or** 3 pieces of stem ginger in syrup, cut into thin strips

Preheat the oven to 180°C fan.

A note on the pie dish: When it comes to your pie dish, the options here are endless. Some people like a deep crumble with lots of fruit on the bottom and a thick layer of crumble on top, while others are the complete opposite and prefer a thin layer of fruit and a thin layer of crumble. I'm somewhere in between. This recipe is written for a 1.2 litre pie dish, the equivalent of which is a 23cm round dish. I often use an oval dish that is 28cm x 16cm.

Arrange the chopped rhubarb in the bottom of your pie dish and sprinkle with the sugar and whichever type of ginger you're using. ➔

For the crumble topping:

100g plain flour

100g porridge oats

100g caster sugar

100g butter, chilled and diced

To serve:

crème fraîche, softly whipped cream, vanilla ice cream or custard (pages 128–130)

For the crumble topping, simply rub all the ingredients together until you have a very crumbly mixture with lots of clusters – my style of crumble topping is slightly more on the biscuity side. Sprinkle the crumble over the fruit.

Bake in the preheated oven for 40–50 minutes, until the crumble is golden and the fruit is bubbling around the edges. I enjoy serving this crumble with some crème fraîche, but softly whipped cream, vanilla ice cream or homemade custard are all good too.

Note

Rhubarb varies widely when it comes to how sweet or sour it is. Taste a little of the raw rhubarb and if it's very sour, use the higher amount of sugar. Forced rhubarb is a lot sweeter than the regular rhubarb available later in the year. Plus the older a plant gets, the more sour the rhubarb will be. My Granny Daisy had rhubarb growing down the end of her garden that was so old and sour that she'd give us a bag of sugar that we'd dip the stalks straight into and eat it raw – not something I'd recommend giving to kids nowadays!

Variations

LET'S GET READY TO CRUMBLE!

The bases, fillings and toppings for tarts and crumbles really are interchangeable and so many combinations are possible. Once you have grasped the basics, you can easily experiment. Why not use a crumble mixture to top your tart or use the apple tart filling for a crumble and vice versa? Use these filling ideas to help you explore even more combinations.

APPLE & BERRY

Add about 150g berries to 500g apples, peeled, cored and thinly sliced. Use whichever berries you like, such as raspberries, blackberries or tayberries. If you haven't tried tayberries yet, please seek them out the next berry season! They are a cross between a blackberry and a red raspberry. They are very aromatic and have a beautiful, sweet raspberry taste without the sharpness you sometimes get from our standard pink raspberries.

RHUBARB & STRAWBERRY

I've been told that strawberries work really well with rhubarb, but I'm allergic to strawberries so I've never tried this one! Use about 150g fresh strawberries to 500g rhubarb.

RHUBARB & MANGO

I love the combination of rhubarb and mango. Use about 150g diced fresh or frozen mango to 500g rhubarb along with the zest of a lime. You could also add some desiccated coconut to the crumble topping.

PEACH

Tinned or fresh peaches make great crumbles and tarts. Add a little flaked almonds if you wish. Use 2 x 400g tins of peaches, drained, or eight fresh peaches, stoned and each one cut into eight wedges.

MINCEMEAT

At Christmas, make it seasonal by pimping up a jar of mincemeat with some fresh apple, chopped dried apricots, chopped roasted nuts and a dash of brandy. This works particularly well with a tart base (see pages 14–15 for the sweet shortcrust pastry) and a crumble topping.

Chocolate, banana & coconut crumble
with banana ice cream

I love pretty much everything served with some softly whipped fresh cream, but this recipe is a rare exception. The contrast of the ice-cold ice cream with the hot pudding works so well, and there is a reason for this. I've written already on page 132 about the different tastes that our mouth can pick up, but this is only part of our sense of taste. Our mouth also factors in the smell, texture and temperature of food as well as coolness (menthol) and hotness (spice). Your sense of taste really is an amazing thing. Use it, enjoy it and don't take it for granted – since the covid pandemic, a lot more of us have realised how unpleasant it is if you lose your sense of taste.

Serves 6

650g bananas (about 6 bananas), peeled and cut in half lengthways

juice of 1 lemon

75g caster sugar

2 chocolate coconut bars (such as Bounty), cut into chunks

50g milk chocolate or dark chocolate chips

First you'll need to freeze the bananas for the ice cream. Peel the four bananas and cut into rounds 5cm thick. Place the pieces on a baking tray lined with non-stick baking paper and pop into the freezer for at least a few hours or overnight, until the bananas are frozen. If you're doing this more than a day in advance, once the bananas are frozen, put them into a freezerproof bag until you want to use them.

Preheat the oven to 180°C fan.

Gently toss the halved bananas with the lemon juice in a large bowl. Arrange half of the bananas in the bottom of your pie dish (see the note on pie dishes on page 140) and sprinkle with the sugar, the chunks of the chocolate coconut bars and the chocolate chips, then arrange the rest of the bananas on top.

For the crumble topping, simply rub all the ingredients together until you have a very crumbly mixture – my style of crumble topping is slightly more on the biscuity side. Sprinkle the crumble over the fruit. ➔

For the crumble topping:

100g plain flour

100g caster sugar

100g butter, chilled and diced

50g desiccated coconut

For the banana ice cream:

4 bananas

a squeeze of honey

2–4 tbsp milk

Bake in the preheated oven for 40–50 minutes, until the crumble topping is golden.

To make the banana ice cream, simply place the frozen bananas, honey and about 2 tablespoons of the milk into a food processor and blitz until smooth, adding a little more milk if required.

Serve the ice cream immediately with the banana crumble while the crumble is still hot to get the best contrast.

Rice pudding, semolina & 'frog spawn'

My mum is an expert at cooking rice pudding. Cooked long and slow, you could sense the anticipation in the house when us kids knew it was coming for dessert. Rice pudding along with its sister recipes of semolina and tapioca (or as we called it, frog spawn!) are classics for a reason and need to be preserved. Their simplicity and comforting nature just cannot be beaten, especially on a cold winter evening.

Serves 4

Rice pudding

butter, for greasing

80g pearl rice or pudding rice

50g caster sugar

600ml milk

200ml cream

1 bay leaf

1 tsp vanilla

¼ tsp ground nutmeg

To serve:

your favourite jam

chilled whipped cream

Preheat the oven to 130°C fan. Grease a 1.2 litre ovenproof dish with butter.

Put all the ingredients in a bowl and stir well, then pour into the greased dish. Bake in the preheated oven for 2 hours 15 minutes. When ready, the pudding will have a brown skin on top and the rice will have swollen and become tender.

Serve hot with some jam and chilled whipped cream.

Semolina
with thyme-roasted peaches

550ml milk

50g semolina

50g caster sugar

20g butter

1 tsp vanilla

¼ tsp ground
cinnamon

For the peaches:

4 ripe peaches, stoned
and quartered

leaves of 1 sprig of
fresh thyme

a drizzle of honey

a splash of water

To serve:

chilled whipped cream

Preheat the oven to 180°C fan.

To roast the peaches, put them in a baking dish. Sprinkle over the thyme leaves and drizzle with honey and a splash of water. Bake in the preheated oven for 20 minutes. (Or if you're in a hurry, simply open a tin of peaches!)

Meanwhile, heat the milk in a saucepan until it's almost reached the boiling point, then sprinkle in the semolina. Bring to the boil and cook for 3–4 minutes, stirring continuously, until thickened. Remove from the heat and stir in the sugar, butter, vanilla and cinnamon.

Allow the peaches to cool slightly before serving with the warm semolina and chilled whipped cream.

Tapioca

50g tapioca

500ml milk

25g caster sugar

your favourite jam

Put the tapioca and milk in a heavy-based saucepan and bring to the boil. Reduce the heat and simmer for 15–20 minutes, stirring frequently to stop it sticking to the pan, until it becomes thick and creamy.

Take the pan off the heat and stir in the sugar. It's ready to serve at this stage, but I like to add a little jam on top, then pour it into a serving dish, sprinkle a little extra sugar on top and brown it under a hot grill.

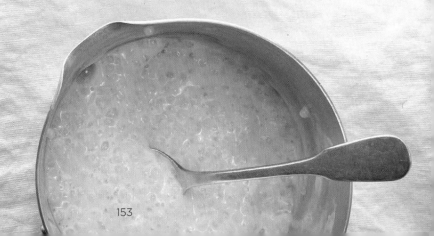

Sholeh zard

Sholeh zard is a Persian rice pudding flavoured with saffron, rosewater and cardamom. My love of Middle Eastern spices continues, as I'm also using advieh in my version. Advieh is a spice blend that includes dried rose, cardamom, cumin, cinnamon and ginger. Normally this dish is served cold, but I like to serve it just warm, as I think it allows the mellow warmth of the spices to really stand out.

Serves 4

150g pearl rice or pudding rice

50g caster sugar

500ml milk

220ml cream

1 strip of orange peel (use a vegetable peeler to peel a strip from an orange)

4 green cardamom pods, lightly crushed

a pinch of saffron

1 tbsp advieh

2 tbsp rosewater

50g cold butter, cubed

1 medium egg yolk

To decorate:

an extra pinch of advieh

roughly chopped pistachios

dried rose petals

orange zest

Put the rice, sugar, milk, cream, orange peel, crushed cardamom pods and saffron in a heavy-based saucepan and gently bring to a simmer. Continue to simmer gently for 30–40 minutes, until thick and creamy, stirring regularly so that it doesn't stick to the bottom of the saucepan.

Remove from the heat and stir in the advieh and rosewater, then stir in the cold butter one piece at a time.

Allow to cool until it's just warm, stirring regularly as this will stop it forming a skin.

Just before serving, remove the whole cardamom pods and orange peel, then stir through the egg yolk. The sholeh zard should have a nice velvety texture. If you feel that it's a bit too thick, stir through a little more cream.

Serve in individual glass bowls and decorate with an extra pinch of advieh, chopped pistachios, dried rose petals and orange zest.

Sherry trifle

There is a bang of the 1970s off this – or in my case, a bang of Christmas Day in the 1980s – but trifle is much older than that. The first record of a trifle dates back to 1585, but that version was a lot different from what we eat today. We have to wait until 1747 and Hannah Glasse's book *The Art of Cookery* before we get a recipe that resembles what we now know as trifle. I wasn't a huge fan of trifle when I was young. It wasn't until the late 1990s, when I tasted a trifle made by the amazing cook Mairead Hutchinson in Gort Muire, that I fell in love with this classic. She made the most amazing trifle and an even better chocolate pudding.

Serves 8–10

For the Swiss roll layer:

1 Swiss roll (page 86 or buy a good shop-bought one – it can be our secret)

4 tbsp sweet sherry (optional)

For the jelly layer:

350g frozen mixed berries

200ml water

1 packet of jelly – raspberry, strawberry and blackcurrant all work really well

For the custard layer:

50g caster sugar

30g cornflour

2 medium egg yolks

1 tsp vanilla

500ml milk

Start by cutting the Swiss roll into slices and arranging them in the bottom of a trifle bowl. Drizzle over the sherry (if using).

For the jelly layer, place the frozen fruit and water in a saucepan and slowly bring to a simmer. Cut the block of jelly into small pieces and add it to the warmed fruit, stirring until the jelly is dissolved. Pour this over the Swiss roll and refrigerate until set.

While the jelly is setting, make the custard. In a large bowl, make a paste with the sugar, cornflour, egg yolks, vanilla and 2 tablespoons milk (taken from the 500ml).

Heat up the rest of the milk in a saucepan. Just before it starts to boil, pour the hot milk into the paste and mix well. Return the mixture to the saucepan and slowly bring to the boil. Once it has reached a boil, remove the pan from the heat. Pour the custard into a clean bowl and press a piece of cling film directly on the surface – this will prevent a skin forming on the custard. Allow to cool completely.

For the whipped cream layer, simply whisk the cream with the icing sugar until it forms soft peaks.

To assemble, pour the cooled custard over the jelly layer before adding the final layer of whipped cream. Decorate with the glacé cherries and angelica.

Keep chilled until ready to serve and scatter over the sprinkles just before serving.

For the whipped cream layer:

500ml cream

25g icing sugar

To decorate:

glacé cherries

angelica (this can be a little hard to find nowadays, but it really adds to the retro feel)

hundreds and thousands (or any other sprinkles)

Triple chocolate brownie trifle

A bit like the brack and butter pudding on page 124, don't be too hard on yourself if you decide to just make the brownie and leave it at that, because believe me, it's a good brownie! If you fancy making something indulgent and showstopping, though, this is it.

Serves 9–12

For the brownie layer:

185g butter, plus extra for greasing

185g dark chocolate chips

85g plain flour

40g cocoa powder

3 medium eggs, beaten

275g caster sugar

50g milk chocolate chips

50g white chocolate chips

For the chocolate custard layer:

50g caster sugar

30g cornflour

15g cocoa powder

2 medium egg yolks

500ml milk

100g milk chocolate chips

Preheat the oven to 160°C fan. Prepare a 23cm square baking tin by lightly greasing it with butter and lining with non-stick baking paper.

Melt the butter in a saucepan until slightly warmed, then remove the pan from the heat. Add the dark chocolate chips, stirring to melt the chocolate and combine it with the butter. Leave to cool to room temperature.

Sift the flour and cocoa powder together and set aside.

Using an electric hand mixer or a stand mixer fitted with the whisk attachment, whisk the eggs and sugar together until they look thick and creamy and have doubled in volume. Pour in the cooled chocolate mixture and gently fold together using a large metal spoon. Add the sifted flour and cocoa powder along with the milk chocolate and white chocolate chips. Gently fold everything together.

Pour the batter into the prepared tin. Bake in the preheated oven for 20–25 minutes. The bake should have a slightly shiny look and the top should feel like a sheet of paper.

Remove from the oven and allow to cool completely in the tin. Keep going to make the trifle or cut the brownies into portions and enjoy them now, just as they are.

To make the chocolate custard, in a large bowl, make a paste with the sugar, cornflour, cocoa powder, egg yolks and 2 tablespoons milk (taken from the 500ml).

Heat up the rest of the milk in a saucepan. Just before it starts to boil, pour the hot milk into the paste and mix well. Return the mixture to the saucepan and slowly bring to the boil. ➲

For the whipped cream layer:

500ml cream

25g icing sugar

4 tbsp Irish cream liqueur, plus extra for assembling (optional)

To decorate:

chocolate pieces, such as Flake, crushed Maltesers or whatever you fancy

Once it has reached a boil, remove the pan from the heat and stir in the chocolate chips until they have melted and everything is evenly combined. Pour the custard into a clean bowl and press a piece of cling film directly on the surface – this will prevent a skin forming on the custard. Allow to cool completely.

For the whipped cream layer, simply whisk the cream with the icing sugar and Irish cream liqueur (if using) until it forms soft peaks.

To assemble, cut the brownie into bite-sized pieces and arrange in the bottom of a trifle bowl, then drizzle with a few tablespoons of the liqueur (if using). Pour the cooled chocolate custard over the brownie before adding the final layer of whipped cream.

Keep chilled until ready to serve. Decorate with the crushed chocolate pieces just before serving.

My childhood *favourites*

Mammy buns
Rice Krispie buns
Milk jelly

For as long as I can remember, I've always referred to buns as 'mammy buns'. That's what our mammy made and if you went to a friend's house as a kid and there were buns, you could be assured they were made by their mammy. But no matter what you call them – fairy cakes, queen cakes, cupcakes or buns – these little classics were a staple growing up, especially at a party along with Rice Krispie buns. When we went to see our Granny Daisy, our treat was jelly. She would always make two pint bowls: one filled with a classic jelly with some fruit in it and the second would be a cloudy milk jelly, which I absolutely loved. If there are younger members of the family, get them involved in making these. We all fondly remember licking the spoon and the sponge mixture in the bowl, don't we?

Mammy buns

Makes 12 large cupcakes or 24 small traditional buns

165g butter, very soft

165g caster sugar

165g self-raising flour

3 medium eggs

1 tsp baking powder

½ tsp vanilla

**To decorate
(choose one):**

jam and desiccated coconut

jam and buttercream frosting (page 12) or whipped cream

buttercream frosting (page 12) and sprinkles

Preheat the oven to 180°C fan. Line your cupcake or bun trays with paper cases (12 cupcake cases or 24 smaller bun cases).

Put all the ingredients in a large bowl. Using an electric hand mixer or a stand mixer fitted with the paddle attachment, mix everything together until you have a smooth, well-combined, fluffy batter. This will take a minute or two.

Divide the batter between the paper cases. Bake in the preheated oven for 18–20 minutes for the larger cupcakes or 14–16 minutes for the smaller buns, until golden brown and a skewer inserted into the middle of each cake comes out clean.

Transfer to a wire rack and leave to cool completely, then decorate as desired:

- Spread a little jam across the top of each bun and roll in desiccated coconut.

- Cut the top off each bun. Decorate with a little jam and frosting or freshly whipped cream. Cut the top in half and place back on the bun to look like butterfly wings.

- Pipe on some buttercream frosting and decorate with sprinkles.

Rice Krispie buns

Makes 12 large or 24 small buns

300g milk chocolate, roughly chopped

150g Rice Krispies

To decorate:

sugar sprinkles or sweets

Line your cupcake or bun trays with paper cases (12 cupcake cases or 24 smaller bun cases).

Put the chocolate in a large heatproof bowl set over a pan of gently simmering water, making sure the water doesn't touch the bottom of the bowl (see page 14 for more info on melting chocolate). Once it has melted, remove the bowl from the pan and stir in the Rice Krispies until evenly combined.

Divide the mixture between the paper cases, pushing down gently. Decorate the top with sprinkles or sweets and allow to set.

Milk jelly

Serves 4

1 x 135g block of jelly (any flavour)

100ml water

400ml full-fat milk, slightly warmed

Melt the jelly with the water in a saucepan set over a medium heat. When the jelly has completely dissolved, add the warm milk and stir well.

Pour into individual glasses or a serving dish and chill in the fridge to set. Importantly, stir the jelly several times during the cooling process to stop the jelly splitting.

My adulthood favourites

Tahini & black sesame cupcakes
Mahleb & orange shortbread
Rose jelly

A lot of people know me as The Cupcake Bloke, the name of the business I started with my husband in 2012, so I couldn't write this book without including at least one cupcake. The business has given me the opportunity to discover who I am, what I want to say regarding food and what my style is. This book is basically a reflection of what I have discovered in the past 10 years: my love of traditional bakes, my love of flavour and my love of reinvention. It might not come as a surprise, but each of my adulthood favourites has a Middle Eastern influence. I must thank chef Aoife Noonan for introducing me to mahleb, an amazing spice made from the kernel of the St Lucie cherry. It has a sweet taste with notes of almond and cherry.

Tahini & black sesame cupcakes

Makes 12

165g self-raising flour

165g caster sugar

115g butter, very soft

50g tahini

3 medium eggs

1 tsp baking powder

½ tsp vanilla

1 tbsp black sesame seeds, plus extra to decorate (see the note)

For the frosting:

100g butter, softened

50g tahini

300g icing sugar

2 tbsp milk (optional)

Preheat the oven to 180°C fan. Line your cupcake tray with paper cases.

Put all the ingredients except the black sesame seeds in a large bowl. Using an electric hand mixer or a stand mixer fitted with the paddle attachment, mix everything together until you have a smooth, well-combined, fluffy batter. This will take a minute or two. Gently fold in the black sesame seeds.

Divide the batter between the paper cases. Bake in the preheated oven for 18–20 minutes, until golden brown and a skewer inserted into the middle of each cake comes out clean.

Transfer to a wire rack and leave to cool completely.

To make the frosting, using an electric mixer or the stand mixer again, mix the softened butter with the tahini and icing sugar, starting slowly or you'll have a big mess! Continue to whisk for about 5 minutes, adding a little milk if you would like to make the frosting a little softer.

Using either a piping bag, a palette knife or a spoon, divide the frosting between the cupcakes. To decorate, sprinkle with more black sesame seeds.

Note

You can get black sesame seeds from Asian food shops.

Rose jelly

Makes 4 servings

1 x 135g packet of
raspberry jelly

100ml water

400ml cream, warmed

2 tbsp rosewater

To decorate:

fresh raspberries

lime zest

chopped pistachios

Melt the jelly with the water in a saucepan set over a medium
heat. When the jelly has completely dissolved, add the warm
cream and rosewater and stir well.

Pour into individual glasses or a serving dish and chill in the
fridge to set. Importantly, stir the jelly several times during
the cooling process to stop the jelly splitting.

Chill completely and decorate with fresh raspberries, a little
lime zest and chopped pistachios before serving.

Mahleb & orange shortbread

Makes 15 biscuits

170g plain flour, plus
extra for dusting

125g butter, chilled
and diced

55g caster sugar, plus
extra for dusting

zest of ½ orange

1 tsp mahleb or
almond extract

Preheat the oven to 150°C fan. Line a baking tray with non-stick
baking paper.

Place all the ingredients in a large bowl. Using your fingers, rub
everything together until it looks like fine breadcrumbs, then squeeze
everything together to form a stiff dough.

Roll the dough out on a lightly floured surface to a thickness of 6mm.
Cut the dough into fingers or use a cutter to stamp out rounds.
Alternatively, if you have a ma'amoul mould (a Middle Eastern cookie
shaper) or any type of cookie press, divide the mixture into 15 equal
pieces and use that.

Place on the prepared baking tray and dust with some extra caster
sugar. Chill in the fridge for 15 minutes.

Bake in the preheated oven for 15–20 minutes, until golden brown.
Allow to cool on the tray for 5 minutes before using a palette knife to
transfer to a wire rack. Allow to cool completely before eating.

Chocolate chip cookies

Do you remember the chocolate chip cookies from the 1980s and early 1990s?. It could have been a Maryland or one of the few that were in the tin of USA or Afternoon Tea biscuits. The ones that stick out in my mind are the ones Mum used to bring home from Dublin in the late 1980s – I think they were from Marks & Spencer. I remember that they were so much bigger than those we were used to and so much more American. This is my take.

Makes 12

160g butter, softened

80g light brown sugar

80g caster sugar

1 medium egg, beaten

1 tbsp milk

225g plain flour

½ tsp bread soda

200g chocolate chips (I like to use a mix of milk and dark chocolate)

Using an electric hand mixer or a stand mixer fitted with the paddle attachment, cream the butter and sugars together until they are light and fluffy. This will take a few minutes.

Add the egg and milk and mix for a further 30 seconds, followed by the flour and bread soda and mix for another 30 seconds.

Next mix in the chocolate chips – I find using a wooden spoon easier for this step.

Divide the mixture into 12 evenly sized portions. Roll each one into a ball between the palms of your hands, flattening them slightly. I like to refrigerate these for 24 hours before baking, but if your cookie craving is too strong, just refrigerate them for 30 minutes. Letting the dough sit for 24 hours allows the starch and proteins in the flour to break down a bit, which leads to a more even bake. Have you ever noticed that when you bake cookies straightaway, they tend to have a thin edge and a domed centre? But when you let the dough sit for a day, the cookies bake more uniformly all over.

Preheat the oven to 160°C fan. Line two baking trays with non-stick baking paper.

Put six cookies on each tray, spacing them well apart. Bake in the preheated oven for 15–18 minutes – they should be slightly brown at the edges and still soft in the centre.

Allow to cool on the tray for a few minutes before transferring to a wire rack.

Note Try adding a pinch of flaky sea salt on
top of your cookies before you bake
them for a sweet 'n' salty hit.

Variations

TWISTED COOKIES

I've taken another classic recipe and added a few savoury and unusual ingredients to take it to the next level. Don't be afraid to do this yourself – one of the best ways to become a better baker is to experiment. The next time you're making the basic chocolate chip cookie recipe on page 174, why not take half the dough and add a few bits of your own? I know you might be thinking I've completely lost the plot with some of these. 'Crisps in a cookie? Is he mad?' I can hear you saying. But don't knock it till you've tried it!

SNICKERS
Replace the chocolate chips with 200g chopped-up Snickers bars. (Keep the Snickers cold – it makes them easier to chop and mix in.) Stud the top of the just-shaped cookies with a few salted peanuts for added crunch, then refrigerate and bake as per the original recipe. This also works well with Mars bars, Smarties and M&M's.

AMARENA CHERRY, HAZELNUT & ORANGE
In addition to the chocolate chips in the original recipe, add 100g Amarena cherries cut into quarters, 25g chopped toasted hazelnuts and the zest of half an orange. This variation will yield 14–16 cookies.

TAYTO CHEESE & ONION
In addition to the chocolate chips, add 1 bag of roughly crushed Tayto cheese and onion crisps (or King crisps if you're from Dublin!).

SMOKED BACON, PRETZEL & DARK CHOCOLATE
Cut 150g smoked streaky bacon into very thin pieces. Cook the bacon in 50g butter until crisp and golden. Use a sieve to separate the bacon from the cooking fat, catching the fat in a small bowl and allowing the fat to cool completely. When measuring the butter for your cookies, start off by using the cooled cooking fat and then making it up to the 160g needed in total with butter. Only use dark chocolate chips (not milk chocolate) and add 50g broken-up pretzels (you want to keep some texture) along with the chocolate chips. Stud the tops of the just-shaped cookies with a whole pretzel, then refrigerate and bake as per the original recipe.

Fifteens

This famous 'fridge bake' from Northern Ireland is so called because of its easy-to-remember ingredients list. Very little is known about the origins of this treat, which seems unique to that part of the world.

Makes 15 slices

15 digestive biscuits

15 glacé cherries, cut in half

15 large pink and white marshmallows, each one cut into 4 (I find a scissors works best for this)

200g condensed milk

75g desiccated coconut

Crush the digestive biscuits in a large bowl, then add the cut cherries and marshmallows. Pour over the condensed milk and mix well.

Lay out a sheet of cling film on the countertop and sprinkle half the coconut on top. Pour the biscuit mixture onto the cling film and shape into a log roughly 30cm long. Sprinkle more coconut on top and wrap the cling film tightly around it.

Chill in the fridge for at least 4 hours, but overnight is even better.

Unwrap from the cling film and cut into – you've guessed it – 15 slices.

Rocky road

I think we've all had a 'rocky road' of some sort at some point in our lives. My rocky road is definitely my journey as a gay man, coming to terms with my sexuality, falling in love, building a life and business, all the way through to civil partnership and finally marriage equality in 2015. I'm so lucky that I've had Daithí by my side for most of that time. I hope that your rocky road has had or will have a happy ending too.

Makes 16 portions

720g dark chocolate, roughly chopped

300g butter, plus extra for greasing

60g golden syrup

200g digestive or rich tea biscuits, broken into bite-sized pieces

150g mini marshmallows

200g mixed sweets, such as M&M's, Smarties and/or jellies, whichever are your favourites

100g other biscuits, such as iced rings or pink wafers, broken into bite-sized pieces

1 tsp sugar sprinkles (optional)

Grease a 23cm square baking tin and line with non-stick baking paper.

Melt the chocolate, butter and golden syrup together in a medium-sized heatproof bowl over a pan of gently simmering water, making sure the water doesn't touch the bottom of the bowl (see page 14 for more info on melting chocolate). Stir until smooth and combined. Remove the bowl from the pan and set aside to cool a little.

Pour one-third of the chocolate mixture over the base of the prepared tin. Scatter the plain biscuits, half of the marshmallows and some of the sweets over the base layer of chocolate.

Pour over half of the remaining chocolate mixture, then shake the tin a little to allow the chocolate to fill any holes or gaps.

Make a second layer with the rest of the biscuits, marshmallows and sweets (reserving a few to scatter over the top), then pour over the remaining chocolate mixture. Shake the tin as before to encourage the chocolate into any holes.

Scatter with the reserved ingredients, then finally scatter over the sprinkles (if using).

Cool in the fridge for at least 4 hours, until it is firmly set, before cutting into squares.

Salt
&
Pepper

Jambons

The jambon is now as Irish as soda bread, so it's only right that it gets its place as a 'traditional' bake (check out 'Mysteries of the Deli: The Jambon' by Caitríona Devery in *District Magazine* online to read more about the history of the jambon).

I grew up living over the family pork butcher shop. My father, along with the two Paddys and Bobby, cooked and made lots of our own products: sausages and puddings as well as cooked meats like ham, hazlet and brawn. They also cooked crubeens at the weekend. I can clearly remember myself and my brother Patrick (Pappy) sitting in the shop hallway eating those gelatinous beauties while they were still warm. But I don't expect you to cook crubeens for this dish; ham hocks give the same flavour. Some retailers cook their own ham hocks and have them available at their hot deli counters, but if you don't want to use ham hock, use thick slices of ham cut into small dice. I know these homemade jambons might seem like a lot of work, but trust me, they're worth it.

Makes 12

20g butter

20g plain flour

200ml milk

150g Cheddar cheese, grated

1 tsp mustard of your choice (optional)

salt and freshly ground black pepper

200g cooked ham hock, torn into small pieces (or see the intro)

1 sheet of ready-rolled puff pastry

1 medium egg, beaten

Start by making the béchamel (white sauce). Melt the butter in a heavy-based saucepan over a medium heat, then stir in the flour and cook for about 2 minutes, stirring constantly so that the flour doesn't burn. Slowly pour in the milk, continuously whisking until it comes to a simmer. Continue cooking and stirring for another 3–4 minutes, until the sauce has thickened, before removing the pan from the heat. Vigorously mix in half of the cheese and all of the mustard (if using) and season with salt and pepper. Allow to cool, then stir in the remaining cheese and the cooked ham hock.

Unroll the sheet of puff pastry and cut it into 12 x 8cm squares. Brush each square with a little of the beaten egg. Divide the filling between the puff pastry squares, using a spoon to put a large mound in the centre of each square.

Fold the four corners up into the centre of the filling and brush with a little more beaten egg. Place on a baking tray lined with non-stick paper and chill in the fridge for 15 minutes.

Preheat the oven to 180°C fan.

Bake in the preheated oven for 20–25 minutes, until fully cooked. Serve warm.

Black & white jambons

This recipe is actually for two separate jambons that celebrate black and white pudding and my fond memories of growing up over our family pork butcher shop. Bobby was the main sausage-, dripping- and pudding-maker in the shop and his puddings were so good. I even have a vague recollection of red pudding being made. Our shop window would be decorated with swags of sausages and rings of puddings. There used to be several Herterich Butchers all over Ireland, from Wexford to Castlebar, but at the time of writing there are only two shops remaining: Herterich's in Longford, which is run by the second and third generation of Louis Herterich, and Herterich's in Galway, run by John Herterich. I visit both whenever I can and there is still a certain pride, fuelled by my childhood memories, in seeing the family name on their shopfronts.

Makes 12

20g butter

20g plain flour

200ml milk

salt and freshly ground black pepper

1 sheet of ready-rolled puff pastry

1 medium egg, beaten

Start by making the béchamel (white sauce). Melt the butter in a heavy-based saucepan over a medium heat, then stir in the flour and cook for about 2 minutes, stirring constantly so that the flour doesn't burn. Slowly pour in the milk, continuously whisking until it comes to a simmer. Continue cooking and stirring for another 3–4 minutes, until the sauce has thickened, before removing the pan from the heat. Season with salt and pepper and allow to cool.

Unroll the sheet of puff pastry and cut it into 12 x 8cm squares. Brush each square with a little of the beaten egg. To fill, start by dividing the béchamel between the 12 squares of pastry. Top with the relevant ingredients depending on whether you're making the black or the white pudding version, building them up in a stack on top of the béchamel.

Fold the four corners up into the centre of the filling and brush with a little more beaten egg. Place on a baking tray lined with non-stick paper and chill in the fridge for 15 minutes.

Preheat the oven to 180°C fan.

Bake in the preheated oven for 20–25 minutes, until fully cooked. Serve warm.

300g black pudding, cut into 12 slices

200g blue cheese, cut into 12 pieces

2 pears, peeled and each cut into 6 wedges

1 leek, sliced and cooked in a little butter

300g white pudding, cut into 12 slices

1 apple, peeled, cored and cut into 12 wedges

200g Brie cheese, cut into 12 pieces

60g shop-bought crispy onions

Sausage rolls

Whenever we made the journey to visit my mum's brother and his wife – Pad and Harriet, who were also my godparents – I would secretly hope that Harriet would whip out a plate of her sausage rolls, which she invariably did. They were always just out of the oven and oh so tasty.

Makes 12

1 tbsp vegetable oil

½ onion, finely diced

¼ tsp dried sage

500g pork mince or sausage meat (I like to use a mix of both)

salt and freshly ground black pepper

1 sheet of ready-rolled puff pastry

plain flour, for dusting

1 medium egg, beaten

shop-bought red pepper relish, to serve

Preheat the oven to 180°C fan. Line two baking trays with non-stick baking paper.

Heat the oil in a frying pan over a medium heat. Add the onion and cook gently for about 10 minutes, until soft, adding the sage just before you take the pan off the heat. Allow to cool.

Put the pork mince and/or sausage meat in a bowl (first removing the skins if using whole sausages) along with the cooled onion. Season with a little salt and pepper and mix well by hand.

Unroll the pastry on a lightly floured work surface and cut it lengthways into two long, even rectangles.

Divide the sausage filling in two. Roll half of the filling into a long sausage shape with your hands along the centre of each rectangle.

Brush the pastry on one side of the filling with the beaten egg, then fold the other side of the pastry over the filling, wrapping it inside. Turn so that the seal is on the bottom of the sausage roll. Cut each long roll into six and space them out on the lined baking trays.

Brush the top of each roll with the beaten egg. Bake in the preheated oven for 25 minutes, until puffed up, golden and cooked through. Serve with red pepper relish on the side.

Pork & fennel rolls
with fennel & apple slaw

I adore the sweet, mild aniseed flavour that comes from fennel. It works really well in both sweet and savoury dishes, and pork with a mix of fresh fennel bulb and fennel seeds is a great combination. The first time I ever had the two together was years ago when myself and Daithí were in Rome and I had some finocchiona (a rich pork and fennel salami from Tuscany) in a restaurant called Hostaria Romana. Closer to home, the Wooded Pig, an Irish family-owned company, makes an extremely tasty pork and fennel salami.

Makes 6

1 tbsp vegetable oil

25g butter

½ onion, thinly sliced

1 fennel bulb, finely sliced (keep any green fronds)

1 tsp fennel seeds, crushed, plus extra for sprinkling on top

600g pork mince or sausage meat (I like to use a mix of both)

salt and freshly ground black pepper

1 sheet of ready-rolled puff pastry

plain flour, for dusting

1 medium egg, beaten

Preheat the oven to 180°C fan. Line two baking trays with non-stick baking paper..

Heat the oil and butter in a frying pan over a medium heat. Add the onion and cook gently for about 5 minutes, until starting to soften. Add the sliced fennel bulb and cook for a further 10 minutes, adding the crushed fennel seeds just before you take the pan off the heat. Allow to cool.

Put the pork mince and/or sausage meat in a bowl (first removing the skins if using whole sausages) along with the cooled onion and fennel. Season with a little salt and pepper and mix well by hand.

Unroll the pastry on a lightly floured work surface and cut it lengthways into two long, even rectangles.

Divide the sausage filling in two. Roll half of the filling into a long sausage shape with your hands along the centre of each rectangle.

Brush the pastry on one side of the filling with the beaten egg, then fold the other side of the pastry over the filling, wrapping it inside. Turn so that the seal is on the bottom of the sausage roll. Cut each long roll into three and space them out on the lined baking trays.

Brush the top of each roll with the beaten egg and sprinkle on some extra fennel seeds. Bake in the preheated oven for 25–30 minutes, until puffed up, golden and cooked through. ⊙➔

For the fennel and apple slaw:

6 tbsp mayonnaise

2 tsp Dijon mustard

juice of 1 lemon

2 fennel bulbs, thinly sliced
(keep any green fronds)

1 apple, peeled, cored and cut
into thin strips

Meanwhile, to make the slaw, mix the mayonnaise, mustard and lemon juice together in a large bowl, then season with salt and some freshly ground black pepper. Add the sliced fennel bulb, apple and any green fennel fronds and stir them into the sauce until evenly coated.

Serve the warm sausage rolls with the slaw on the side.

Boxty

A fantastic and tasty way to use up leftover mashed potatoes, boxty is often served as a side dish. The baking powder wouldn't be traditional in the recipe, but I find that it helps make the boxty that little bit lighter. I love to serve these traditional Irish 'pancakes' with sour cream, crispy smoked bacon lardons and some spring onions.

Makes 12 small pancakes

250g raw grated potato

Place the grated potato in the centre of a clean cloth or tea towel and wring out as much moisture as possible.

250g cold mashed potato

100g plain flour

½ tsp baking powder

Mix both the cold mashed potato and the raw grated potato together in a mixing bowl. Add the flour, baking powder, some salt and pepper and enough milk to form a batter of a dropping consistency.

salt and freshly ground black pepper

125ml milk

Heat a little oil in a frying pan over a medium heat and add a little butter. When the butter has melted and starts to foam, add large spoonfuls of the batter to the pan, spreading them out slightly. Don't crowd the pan, as that would lower the temperature of the pan and cause the boxty to go soggy.

vegetable oil, for pan-frying

Cook to a golden brown colour on each side. Keep each batch warm in a low oven while you cook the rest.

a knob of butter

Serve warm in a stack of three topped with sour cream, smoked bacon and sliced spring onions.

To serve:

sour cream

cooked smoked bacon

spring onions, thinly sliced at an angle

Sweet potato & kimchi boxty

Sometimes it takes a few tries to really like and appreciate the flavour of something, and kimchi was one of those things for me. This spicy ferment can be an acquired taste but stick with it because it will become addictive, and if you're like me, you will soon have it with everything. There are several Irish-made kimchis available now and they are a good place to start if you haven't had kimchi before, as they are usually a little less 'funky'. But if and when you do get into kimchi, be sure to try it in a toasted cheese sandwich – delicious.

Makes 12 small pancakes

250g cold mashed sweet potato

250g raw grated sweet potato

150g plain flour

50g kimchi, finely sliced, plus extra to serve

½ tsp baking powder

salt and freshly ground black pepper

100ml milk

vegetable oil, for pan-frying

a knob of butter

To serve:

fried eggs

gochugaru (see the note)

Kewpie mayo (see the note)

hot sauce

Mix both the cold mashed sweet potato and the raw grated sweet potato together in a mixing bowl. Add the flour, kimchi, baking powder, some salt and pepper and enough milk to form a batter of a dropping consistency.

Heat a little oil in a frying pan over a medium heat and add a little butter. When the butter has melted and starts to foam, add large spoonfuls of the batter to the pan, spreading them out slightly. Don't crowd the pan, as that would lower the temperature of the pan and cause the boxty to go soggy.

Cook to a golden brown colour on each side. Keep each batch warm in a low oven while you cook the rest.

Serve warm in a stack of three topped with extra kimchi, a fried egg seasoned with gochugaru, some Kewpie mayonnaise and your favourite hot sauce.

Note

Kewpie mayonnaise is a Japanese mayo made using rice vinegar. It has a slightly more umami flavour than regular mayo. Gochugaru is a Korean red chilli powder.

Mushroom quiche
with pickled enoki

When I was training to be a chef in Waterford, I had a lecturer named Mrs Murphy who always gave out to me for using too much black pepper when seasoning mushrooms. I still do – I am obsessed with the combination. Add some leeks, garlic, the scent of thyme and an amazing sheep's cheese like Cáis na Tíre or Rockfield and you're in for a taste sensation. This is one of those dishes that is best served just warm, not straight out of the oven and definitely not out of the fridge. It's far from pickled enoki mushrooms we were raised, but they're perfect for cutting through the richness of the dish. If you can't find enoki mushrooms, small button mushrooms, sliced, work just as well. I like to serve this quiche with a simple salad of peppery rocket – yes, even more peppery flavour!

Serves 6–8

plain flour, for dusting

1 batch of plain shortcrust pastry (pages 14–15)

500g mushrooms (any variety)

1½ tbsp vegetable oil

60g butter, plus extra for greasing

2 leeks, washed and thinly sliced

3 garlic cloves, finely chopped

2 sprigs of fresh thyme

Grease a 23cm loose-bottomed tart tin and dust with flour.

Place the pastry on a lightly floured surface and roll out to a circle measuring roughly 28cm in diameter. Carefully lift the pastry into the tin and gently press it into the corners and up the sides. Use a sharp knife to trim off any excess pastry. Place the unbaked tart in the fridge to chill for 30 minutes.

Preheat the oven to 180°C fan.

To blind bake the pastry, take a sheet of non-stick baking paper that is big enough to line the bottom and sides of the tin and scrunch it into a ball several times. This makes the paper a lot more pliable and it will fit better into the corners. Cover the pastry base with the paper and fill with uncooked rice or dried beans. Bake in the preheated oven for 20 minutes, then take the tart shell out of the oven and remove the rice or beans and the paper (keep the cooled rice or beans in a container for the next time you need to blind bake something). Return to the oven and bake for another 15 minutes. Allow to cool for 10 minutes on a wire rack. ➔

salt and freshly ground
black pepper

4 medium eggs,
beaten

200ml cream

100ml milk

150g cheese, grated
(I love to use a sheep's
cheese for this recipe,
but feel free to use any
Cheddar or semi-hard
cheese)

For the pickled enoki:

100g enoki
mushrooms, (or small
button mushrooms,
sliced)

100ml white wine
vinegar

2 garlic cloves, slightly
crushed

1 sprig of fresh thyme

½ tbsp caster sugar

To serve:

dressed rocket salad

To prepare your mushrooms for cooking, use a pastry brush to brush off any soil, then depending on the type of mushroom you're using, either cut or tear them into bite-sized pieces. I would cut mushrooms like button, chestnut, shiitake or Paris brown and tear varieties like oyster or hen of the woods.

To make the filling, heat ½ tablespoon of the oil and 20g of the butter in a frying pan over a medium heat. Add the leeks and gently cook for about 8 minutes, then add the garlic and cook for a further 2 minutes, until softened. Remove from the pan and set aside.

Turn up the heat and cook the mushrooms in two batches, using ½ tablespoon of oil, 20g of butter and a sprig of thyme each time. Season each batch with salt and pepper (in my opinion, plenty of the latter!). Don't move the mushrooms too much in the pan, as this will cause them to release a lot of moisture. Instead, let the mushrooms cook untouched until they have a golden colour, then shake the pan. Repeat this several times. Transfer the cooked mushrooms to a plate.

Mix the eggs, cream and milk in a jug and season with salt and pepper.

To fill the quiche, first put the base on a baking tray to make it easier to transfer to the oven. Next arrange the leeks on the bottom of the blind baked quiche base, followed by half of the grated cheese. Add the mushrooms and finally the rest of the cheese. Carefully pour the eggy mixture over the filling and bake in the preheated oven for 30–35 minutes, until golden and just set – the centre shouldn't feel too firm.

Meanwhile, to pickle the enoki muhrooms, put them in a heatproof bowl. Put the vinegar, garlic, thyme and sugar in a small saucepan and bring to the boil, then pour this over the mushrooms. Allow to pickle for 20 minutes before using.

Allow the quiche to cool slightly before cutting into slices and serving with the enoki pickles and dressed rocket. A little of the pickling brine mixed with a drizzle of olive oil is perfect for dressing the rocket.

Full Irish quiche

What I really want to show you here is how versatile quiche is – it's a great way to use leftover bits and pieces. In this recipe I'm using the leftovers from a full Irish fry, but with a little imagination the possibilities are endless. I've included some of my other favourite filling combinations on pages 204–205 and I've named each layer to make it easier for you to try your own combinations.

Serves 6–8

plain flour, for dusting

1 batch of plain shortcrust pastry (pages 14–15)

4 medium eggs, beaten

200ml cream

100ml milk

salt and freshly ground black pepper

The base layer:

1 x 200g tin of baked beans

The cheese layer:

150g Cheddar cheese, grated

The middle layer:

500g cooked breakfast products, such as sausage, bacon, black or white pudding, mushrooms, etc.

To serve:

lightly dressed mixed leaf salad

warm potato salad

Grease a 23cm loose-bottomed tart tin and dust with flour.

Place the pastry on a lightly floured surface and roll out to a circle measuring roughly 28cm in diameter. Carefully lift the pastry into the tin and gently press it into the corners and up the sides. Use a sharp knife to trim off any excess pastry. Place the unbaked tart in the fridge to chill for 30 minutes.

Preheat the oven to 180°C fan.

To blind bake the pastry, take a sheet of non-stick baking paper that is big enough to line the bottom and sides of the tin and scrunch it into a ball several times. This makes the paper a lot more pliable and it will fit better into the corners. Cover the pastry base with the paper and fill with uncooked rice or dried beans. Bake in the preheated oven for 20 minutes, then take the tart shell out of the oven and remove the rice or beans and the paper (keep the cooled rice or beans in a container for the next time you need to blind bake something). Return to the oven and bake for another 15 minutes. Allow to cool for 10 minutes on a wire rack.

Mix the eggs, cream and milk in a jug and season with salt and pepper.

To fill the quiche, put the base on a baking tray to make it easier to transfer to the oven. Next arrange the baked beans on the bottom of the blind baked quiche base, followed by half of the grated cheese. Add the cooked breakfast bits and finally the rest of the cheese. Carefully pour the eggy mixture over the filling and bake in the preheated oven for 30–35 minutes, until golden and just set – the centre shouldn't feel too firm.

Allow to cool slightly before serving. I love to serve this quiche with a simple mixed leaf salad and warm potato salad – cook some baby potatoes (I love to roast them) and allow to cool a little before dressing with some mayonnaise, wholegrain mustard, chopped spring onions and salt and pepper.

Quiche

I LOVE IT WHEN
A PLAN COMES
TOGETHER!

BROCCOLI, SMOKED SALMON & BRIE

1 **The base layer:** 1 medium onion, cooked in a little oil and butter
2 **The middle layer:** 400g broccoli florets (cooked) and 100g smoked salmon, cut into thin strips
3 **The cheese layer:** 150g Brie, cut into small chunks

HAM, PEA, FETA & MINT

1 **The base layer:** 1 medium onion, cooked in a little oil and butter
2 **The middle layer:** 350g cooked ham, torn into strips, 150g frozen peas or petit pois (cooked) and about 6 fresh mint leaves, cut into thin strips (chiffonade)
3 **The cheese layer:** 150g feta cheese, crumbled

TURKEY, CRANBERRY & STUFFING
(PERFECT FOR CHRISTMAS LEFTOVERS)

The base layer: 2 tablespoons cranberry sauce

The middle layer: 350g cooked diced turkey and 150g stuffing

The cheese layer: 150g Cheddar cheese, grated

CAULIFLOWER CHEESE

The base layer: Brush the base of the pastry with a little Dijon mustard

The middle layer: 500g cooked cauliflower florets

The cheese layer: 250g grated cheese (a mature Cheddar is best)

BLUE CHEESE, PEAR, LEEK & WALNUT

The base layer: 1 large or 2 small leeks, cooked in a little oil and butter

The middle layer: 3 ripe pears, peeled, cored and cut into wedges, and 100g walnut pieces

The cheese layer: 250g crumbled blue cheese

Honey & mustard baked ham

There is something about the smell of a baked ham wafting around the house that seems to call out 'eat me, eat me!' and it is so hard to avoid doing just that. My favourite way to eat baked ham is cold, thickly cut, on some of my rye, ale and honey bread (page 28) with butter, sliced gherkins and spiced mayo.

Serves 10–12

4–5kg ham joint, raw

whole cloves

50g honey

50g mustard (English or Dijon)

50g dark brown sugar

To serve:

rye, ale and honey bread (page 28)

softened butter

sliced gherkins

spiced mayo (see the note)

Soak the ham in a large pot of cold water for about 4 hours, changing the water once. Drain.

Cook the ham by covering it with fresh water and bringing it to the boil. Reduce to a simmer and allow for the following cooking time: 40 minutes per kg plus an additional 20 minutes. That means a 4kg ham would take 3 hours to cook, while a 5kg ham would take 3 hours 40 minutes.

When the ham is cooked, allow it to stand in the water for about 10 minutes before removing and allowing to cool slightly. Place on a foil-lined baking tray.

Preheat the oven to 180°C fan.

When the ham is cool enough to handle, use a sharp knife to remove the skin, leaving a layer of fat behind that's 1–2cm thick. Using the same sharp knife, cut a diamond pattern into the fat and stud each cross with a whole clove.

Mix the honey, mustard and brown sugar together in a bowl, then spread half of the glaze over the clove-studded ham. Bake in the preheated oven for 15 minutes, then baste with the rest of the glaze. Return to the oven and bake for a further 15 minutes, until a golden colour all over.

Allow to cool slightly before serving with rye, ale and honey bread, butter, sliced gherkins and some spiced mayo.

Note

For the spiced mayo, simply mix a few tablespoons of mayonnaise with a generous teaspoon of mustard, a squeeze of honey and ½ teaspoon sweet spice (page 15) or mixed spice.

Buckfast baked ham
with pomegranate & mint

This recipe is dedicated to and inspired by Jess Murphy. Jess is the amazing chef at Kai in Galway who supports and encourages so many people – and is renowned for her many creative uses of Buckfast. She continues to inspire me daily, not only to be a better baker, but to be the kind of person who never stops learning and reaching for new stars.

Serves 10–12

4–5kg smoked ham joint, on the bone, raw

1 x 750ml bottle of Buckfast, keeping back 2 tbsp for the final step

1 small bunch of fresh mint, leaves shredded finely (keep the stalks)

50g pomegranate molasses

1 fresh pomegranate, seeds removed

Soak the ham in a large pot of cold water for about 4 hours, changing the water once. Drain.

Cook the ham by pouring in three-quarters of the bottle of Buckfast and topping up with enough fresh water to cover the ham. Throw in the mint stalks and bring to the boil, then reduce to a simmer and allow for the following cooking time: 40 minutes per kg plus an additional 20 minutes. That means a 4kg ham would take 3 hours to cook, while a 5kg ham would take 3 hours 40 minutes.

When the ham is cooked, allow it to stand in the water for about 10 minutes before removing and allowing to cool slightly. Place on a foil-lined baking tray.

Preheat the oven to 180°C fan.

Put the remaining Buckfast (minus the 2 tablespoons that you're saving for the very end) in a small saucepan and bring to the boil, then continue to let it boil until it has reduced by half. Remove the pan from the heat and stir in the pomegranate molasses and half of the shredded mint.

When the ham is cool enough to handle, use a sharp knife to remove the skin, leaving a layer of fat behind that's 1–2cm thick. Using the same sharp knife, cut a diamond pattern into the fat.

Brush half of the Buckfast glaze over the ham. Bake in the preheated oven for 15 minutes, then baste with the rest of the glaze. Return to the oven and bake for a further 15 minutes, until a golden colour all over.

Allow to cool slightly before carving. Serve warm with a simple accompaniment made by mixing the pomegranate seeds with the rest of the mint and the last 2 tablespoons of Buckfast.

Index